The Andrew R. Cecil Lectures on
Moral Values in a Free Society

established by

The University of Texas at Dallas

Volume VII

Previous Volumes of the Andrew R. Cecil Lectures
on Moral Values in a Free Society

Volume I: The Third Way (1979)
Volume II: The Ethics of Citizenship (1980)
Volume III: Conflict and Harmony (1981)
Volume IV: The Search for Justice (1982)
Volume V: The Citizen and His Government (1983)
Volume VI: Our Freedoms: Rights and
    Responsibilities (1984)
The Foundations of a Free Society
    by Andrew R. Cecil

A MELTING POT OR
A NATION OF MINORITIES

A Melting Pot or a Nation of Minorities

ROBERT L. PAYTON
DANIEL K. INOUYE
JOHN HOPE FRANKLIN
HARVEY C. MANSFIELD, JR.
STANLEY M. JOHANSON
ANDREW R. CECIL

With an Introduction by
ANDREW R. CECIL

Edited by
W. LAWSON TAITTE
The University of Texas at Dallas
1986

Library of Congress Catalog Card Number 86-50210
International Standard Book Number 0-292-75096-X

Distributed by the University of Texas Press,
Box 7819, Austin, Texas 78712

FOREWORD

During the week of November 13-20, 1985, The University of Texas at Dallas presented the seventh annual Andrew R. Cecil Lectures on Moral Values in a Free Society, a series that has become an important tradition on our campus since it was established in 1979. As in previous years, statesmen and scholars of national prominence came to share with the academic community and the public their carefully weighed ideas concerning the moral values on which our country was built. This series offers a unique forum for the analysis and debate of such values, and in offering it, the University is fulfilling its responsibility to see that these values are understood and preserved.

The lectures are named for Dr. Andrew R. Cecil, the University's Distinguished Scholar in Residence and the Chancellor Emeritus of The Southwestern Legal Foundation. As President of the Foundation, his leadership of that institution gained him the highest respect in educational and legal circles throughout the United States. When he became Chancellor Emeritus of the Foundation, Dr. Cecil consented to serve as Distinguished Scholar in Residence at The University of Texas at Dallas. The Lectures on Moral Values in a Free Society are aptly named for a man who, throughout his career, has consistently been concerned with the moral verities, always stressing a faith in the dignity and worth of every individual.

The 1985 lectures addressed a question of central importance to our nation at this moment in its history: "The United States: A Melting Pot or a Nation of Minorities?" The five persons who joined Dr. Cecil brought unique perspectives to their consideration of this topic. Three of them enjoy most distinguished academic careers, one is President of a major foundation and has served both as university president and as United States Ambassador, and one is a United States Senator. We are most grateful to Senator Inouye, to Mr. Payton, to Professors Franklin, Mansfield, and Johanson, and to Dr. Cecil for their willingness to share their ideas and for the thoughtful lectures that are preserved in this volume.

U.T. Dallas also wishes to express its appreciation to all those who have helped make the lectures an important part of the life of the University, especially to the supporters of the program. Through their contribution to the Cecil Lectures, these donors enable us to continue this important project and to publish the proceedings of the series, thus ensuring a wide and permanent audience for the ideas they contain.

I am confident that all those who read the lectures published in the seventh volume of the Andrew R. Cecil Lectures on Moral Values in a Free Society, *A Melting Pot or a Nation of Minorities*, will be challenged to give additional thought to the vital issues they address.

ROBERT H. RUTFORD, President
The University of Texas at Dallas
February, 1986

CONTENTS

INTRODUCTION

by

Andrew R. Cecil

William Story, in tribute to his father, Joseph Story (1779-1845), the Associate Justice of the Supreme Court, proudly stated that America "naturalizes the people of all nations who seek its protection, thereby creating a composite people." The large number of ethnic minorities that this country has welcomed makes us what President John F. Kennedy called "this nation of immigrants." For the more than two centuries of our history, it has been the American dream that this vast array of cultures and heritages should somehow blend into one new entity. The American dream has been to become the "melting pot" in which a multitude of ethnic and cultural identities are fused into a single nation.

This dream, however, has never been fully realized. In order to forge the thirteen colonies into one nation, the framers of the Constitution compromised the principle of equality—which had been enshrined so nobly in the Declaration of Independence in the famous phrase "all men are created equal"—with its antithesis, slavery. The consequences of this compromise have created the stresses between ethnic groups that have been recognized and called our "American dilemma." Justice Thurgood Marshall, the first black

member of the Supreme Court, pointed out this "dilemma" in his opinion concurring in part and dissenting in part in the well-known *Bakke* case, when he
wrote, "It is unnecessary in 20th-century America to
have individual Negroes demonstrate that they have
been victims of racial discrimination; the racism of our
society has been so pervasive that none, regardless of
wealth or position, has managed to escape its impact."
(*Regents of the University of California v. Bakke*, 438
U.S. 265, 400, 98 S.Ct. 2733, 2804 [1978].)

Discriminatory systems have affected not only social and political relations in this country but have also
resulted in economic inequities. Minorities, until
recently, have not participated to any measurable extent, for instance, in our total business system. The
1975 report prepared by the House Subcommittee on
SBA Oversight and Minority Enterprise observed
that while minority persons comprise about 16 percent of the nation's population, of the 13 million
businesses in the United States, only 382,000, or approximately 3.0 percent, are owned by minority individuals. In the early seventies, the gross receipts of
all businesses in this country totaled $2,540.8 billion;
of this amount only $16.6 billion, or about 0.65 per-
cent, was realized by minority business concerns.
(H.R. Rep No. 94-468, pp. 1-2 [1975].)

Racism has always been, and still remains, inconsistent with equality of rights as they pertain to citizenship and with the personal liberty which ought to be
enjoyed by everyone within this free land of ours.
Efforts toward the abolishment of racism in our institutions were made by the so-called Civil War
Amendments to the Constitution, which decreed that

civil freedom in this country is universal, without respect to race. Since the validity of the Emancipation Proclamation, issued under the war powers of the President, was questioned, to remove any legal doubts the Thirteenth Amendment was adopted on December 18, 1865, to strike down the institutions of slavery and involuntary service everywhere in the United States.

It was followed by the Fourteenth Amendment when the Thirteenth Amendment proved insufficient and the conviction grew among the statesmen who conducted the federal government that, as it was expressed by the Supreme Court, "something more was necessary in the way of constitutional protection to the unfortunate race who had suffered so much." Hence the Fourteenth Amendment, which made the Negro not only a citizen of the United States but also of the state of his residence, was adopted. While this amendment was intended primarily for the benefit of the Negro race, it also conferred the right of citizenship upon persons of all other races born and naturalized in the United States.

The Fourteenth Amendment was adopted to insure that every person must be treated equally by each state regardless of the color of his skin, but that promise was strangled in its infancy. Almost a century passed before the states and the federal government were finally directed to eliminate all detrimental classifications based on race. After the long dormancy of the Equal Protection Clause, the Congress and the U.S. Supreme Court embarked on the crucial mission of assuring to all persons "the protection of equal laws."

Senator Hubert Humphrey, discussing the purpose of Title VI of the Civil Rights Act of 1964, said: "The bill has a simple purpose. That purpose is to give fellow citizens—Negroes—the same rights and opportunities that white people take for granted. This is no more than what was preached by the prophets, and by Christ Himself. It is no more than what our Constitution guarantees." (110 Cong. Rec. 655 [1964].) The push for equality initiated by the legislative branch of the government was paralleled by decisions in the judicial branch. One such decision of the Supreme Court stated: "Distinctions between citizens solely because of their ancestry are by their very nature odious to free people whose institutions are founded upon the doctrine of equality." (*Hirabayashi v. United States*, 320 U.S. 81, 100, 63 S.Ct. 1375, 1385 [1943].)

The progress made in our nation in confronting the legacy of slavery and racial discrimination is best illustrated by comparing the opinions of the U.S. Supreme Court concerning race relations in the cases of *Scott v. Sandford* in 1856, *Plessy v. Ferguson* in 1895, and *Brown v. Board of Education of Topeka* in 1954.

In 1856 in the case of *Dred Scott v. John F. A. Sandford* (19 How. 393-638, 15 L. Ed. 691 [1857]), the Court declared that the Missouri Compromise—which prohibited slavery in the portion of Louisiana Purchase Territory north of Missouri—was unconstitutional because it deprived slave owners of their property without due process. The matter at issue before the Court was whether descendants of Africans who were imported to this country and sold as slaves could become citizens of the United States when they were emancipated or born of parents who had become free before their births. (The plaintiff was a citizen of the state of Missouri.) Chief Justice Taney delivered the opinion of the Court that they could not become citizens of the United States. They were not included, stated the Court, "and were not intended to be included under the word 'citizens' in the Constitution, and can, therefore, claim none of the rights and privileges which that instrument provides for and secures to citizens of the United States."

The Court took the position that the Negroes, descendants of slaves, were a subordinate and "inferior class" of beings, and, whether emancipated or not, did not have a claim to the rights and privileges of "the people of the United States," who held the power and conducted the government through their representatives. In the opinion of the Court, the men who framed the Declaration of Independence intended to perpetuate the "impassable barrier" between the white race and the whole "enslaved African race" (including mulattoes). The Court further concluded that Negroes are "altogether unfit to associate with the white race, either in social or political relations; and so far inferior, that they had no rights which the white man was bound to respect. . . ." (*Id.*, at 407.) No state law, therefore, passed after the Constitution was adopted, could give any right of United States citizenship to members of the "enslaved African race," although individual states were (as the opinion recognized) competent to confer on such persons state citizenship effective within the state's boundaries.

This position of the Court was challenged by many

prominent lawyers in pursuit of justice. Mr. Justice
Curtis in a dissenting opinion stressed that the Constitution of the United States was established by the
people of the United States through the action, in
each state, of those persons who were qualified by its
laws to act thereon, in behalf of themselves and all
other citizens of the state. In some of the states,
members of the African race were among those
qualified by law to act on this subject. "It would be
strange," wrote Justice Curtis, "if we were to find in
the Constitution anything which deprived of their citizenship any part of the people of the United States
who were among those by whom it was established."

As to the intention of the men who framed the Declaration of Independence, Justice Curtis believed
that—because of their strong belief in the universal
truth that all men are created equal and are endowed
by their Creator with unalienable rights, and because
of the individual opinions they expressed and actions
they undertook—"it would be not just to them, nor
true in itself, to allege that they intended to say that
the Creator of all men had endowed the white race
exclusively, with the great natural rights which the
Declaration of Independence asserts."

In 1896, nearly a half-century later and thirty years
after the adoption of the constitutional amendments
which had clarified the status of black Americans as
citizens, the United States Supreme Court reviewed
the constitutionality of an act of the General Assembly
of the State of Louisiana, passed in 1890, providing
for separate railway carriages for the white and colored races. The constitutionality of this act was chal-

lenged on the grounds that it conflicted with both the Thirteenth Amendment to the Constitution, which abolished slavery, and the Fourteenth Amendment, which prohibits certain restrictive legislation on the part of the states. The Court, by applying the doctrine of "separate but equal," found that the Statute of Louisiana, Acts of 1890, Number 111, was not in conflict with the Constitution.

The Court took the position that the object of the Fourteenth Amendment was to enforce equality of the two races before the law, but it was not intended to abolish distinctions based upon color or to enforce social, as distinguished from political equality, "or commingling of the two races upon terms unsatisfactory to either." Ignoring totally the reality of the sentiments caused by separation of the two races, the Court remarked: "We consider the underlying fallacy of the plaintiff's argument to consist in the assumption that the enforced separation of the two races stamps the colored race with a badge of inferiority. If this be so, it is not by reason of anything found in the act, but solely because the colored race chooses to put that constriction upon it." (163 U.S. 536, 551, 16 S.Ct. 1138, 1143 [1896].)

The Court held that it was within the competency of the state legislatures in exercising their police powers to establish laws permitting separation of the two races in places where they were liable to be brought into contact. The common instances of the valid exercise of such legislative power were the establishment of separate schools for white and colored children and the separation of the two races in theaters and railway carriages. Such separation, according to the Court, did not stamp the colored race with the stigma of inferiority.

In the *Plessy* case, the Court suggested that legislatures were powerless to eradicate racial instincts or to abolish distinctions based upon physical differences, "and the attempt to do so can only result in accentuating the difficulties" in race relations. According to the "separate but equal" doctrine applied by the Court, the government had performed all of the functions respecting "social advantages with which it is endowed" when it has secured to each of its citizens equal rights before the law and equal opportunities for improvement and progress. "If," stated the Court, "the civil and political rights of both races be equal one cannot be inferior to the other civilly or politically. If one race is inferior to the other socially, the Constitution of the United States cannot put them upon the same plane."

The famous dissent by Mr. Justice Harlan in this case was the voice of natural law, or natural justice, protesting the injustice of the "separate but equal" doctrine and its inconsistency with the Constitution of the United States. The Thirteenth and Fourteenth amendments, he claimed, decreed universal civil freedom in this country and removed the race line from our governmental system. "The white race deems itself to be the dominant race in this country," he wrote,

"But in view of the Constitution, in the eye of the law, there is in this country no superior, dominant class of citizens. There is no caste here. Our Constitution is color-blind, and neither knows nor tolerates classes. In respect of civil rights, all citizens are equal before the law. The humblest is the peer of the most powerful. The law regards man as man, and takes no account of his surroundings or of his color when the civil rights as guaranteed by the supreme law of the land are involved." (*Ibid.*, at 558.)

For another half-century, the American courts labored with the doctrine of "separate but equal" without an attempt to reexamine the doctrine in its application to public education. Only in 1954 in the case of *Brown v. Board of Education of Topeka* did the Supreme Court decide to reconsider the question whether segregation of children in public schools solely on the basis of race—even though the physical facilities and other "tangible" factors might have been equal—deprived children of the minority group of equal educational opportunities. The Court stated that it did and concluded that in the field of public education the doctrine of "separate but equal" had no place. Mr. Chief Justice Warren, who delivered the opinion of the Court, wrote:

"To separate school children from others of similar age and qualifications solely because of their race generates a feeling of inferiority as to their status in the community that may affect their hearts and minds in a way unlikely ever to be undone. . . .

"Whatever may have been the extent of psychological knowledge at the time of *Plessy v. Ferguson*, this finding is amply supported by modern authority. Any language in *Plessy v. Ferguson* contrary to this finding is rejected." (347 U.S. 483, 494-495, 74 S.Ct. 686, 691-692 [1954].)

Decisions of the Courts are reversed as our perceptions of justice and natural rights develop. In our search for a truth that may be discovered by reason and revelation, we are far from claiming that the *Brown* decision or subsequent civil-rights legislation offers an absolute solution to the problem of race relations in the United States. The question of highest order is, can the remedies offered for "historic discrimination" bring minority groups into the mainstream of American life?

As Robert L. Payton points out in "Demographics, Democracy, and Education" in opening the 1985 Lectures on Moral Values in a Free Society, the issue of the integration of minorities into the mainstream of American life looms as one of the most important confronting our nation. The United States has succeeded as a "melting pot" in the past in part because the disparate elements it united were relatively homogeneous. Until recently most immigrants to the United States were of European origin; the principal exception was the black population largely brought to this country by force, and it has posed the greatest challenge to the ideal of integrating all elements of society into a single political and social fabric.

Mr. Payton points out that the non-European elements in our society are the fastest-growing components of the population. Ethnic groups that trace their origins to Africa, Latin America, and Asia will continue to play an ever more important role in

American culture and society. This is only one of the demographic changes of great significance to the country—others include the changing median age of the population and the decreasing number of nuclear families that conform to the classic pattern in which both parents care for children until their maturity. Mr. Payton notes that the challenges of a multiracial, multicultural society are not unique to the United States—countries all over the world are finding that the nation-state must learn to accommodate a multiplicity of ethnic, linguistic, religious, and cultural elements.

Senator Daniel K. Inouye in his lecture "Our Constitution: Will It Survive Another 200 Years?" expresses a concern that the rising numbers and political power of the growing nonwhite minorities may pose a threat to the historical ability of our nation to accommodate new groups. A growing disparity between educational achievements of the majority and minorities, the growing percentage of minority soldiers in our all-volunteer army, and a deepening split between white and minority voters all constitute signals of alarm. Senator Inouye sees the great hope of our nation in a commitment to opportunity for all, and judges that only with such a commitment can our Constitution, and our pride in our nation, survive.

Professor John Hope Franklin traces the history of the black minority of our nation in its quest for full civil and political equality in his lecture, "Equality in America: Democracy's Challenge." He notes that the first great opportunity for establishing such equality, the American Revolution, was missed. Throughout our history, the most famous national leaders have

failed in many cases to take up the standards of liberty
and civil rights. It has often been left to little-known
and oppressed individuals to argue their own causes.

In assessing the progress that has been made in the
area of civil rights, Professor Franklin points out that
in areas in which the goal of equality has most nearly
been reached—in sports, in some areas of educational
and political life, in some areas of commerce and business—the results have been gratifying. Such results
could not have come about, in Professor Franklin's
view, without the commitment of such institutions as
churches, schools, and civic organizations and without
a role being taken by the government.

The use of racial preference, advocated by some as
a tool for achieving the objective of remedying past
discrimination, raises the question whether the
Fourteenth Amendment permits preferential treatment of racial minorities as a means of remedying past
discrimination. A "preferred" status for a particular
racial or ethnic minority entails resentment on the
part of persons who are denied equal rights and opportunities on the basis of membership in the
"dominant majority." (It may be noted that the "majority" is composed of various minority groups which
may claim a history of prior discrimination based upon
religious and/or national origin, such as Jews, Catho-
lics, Poles, Italians, and other religious and ethnic
groups.)

Justice Powell, who announced the judgment of the
Court in the *Bakke* case, stressed the serious
problems of justice raised by the idea of preference
itself. There is a certain measure of inequity, the
Court has stated, in forcing innocent persons to bear

the burden of redressing grievances not of their making or to suffer otherwise impermissible burdens in order to enhance the standing of certain ethnic groups. Furthermore, wrote Justice Powell, "preferential programs may only reinforce common stereotypes holding that certain groups are unable to achieve success without special protection based on a factor having no relationship to individual worth." (*Bakke*, 438 U.S. 265, 298, 98 S.Ct. 2733, 2752 [1978].) The guarantees of the Fourteenth Amendment extend to all persons, and the rights created by the first section of the amendment are personal rights. According to the decision in the *Bakke* case, "The guarantee of equal protection cannot mean one thing when applied to one individual and something else when applied to a person of another color. If both are not accorded the same protection, then it is not equal."

Professor Harvey Mansfield, Jr., addresses some of the issues involved in this "idea of preference" in his lecture "Affirmative Action *versus* the Constitution." He approaches the problem by considering the question of its wisdom for the society as a whole and, more specifically, its probable effects on those whom the remedies are intended to benefit—most specifically on the black Americans who have systematically been denied their rights for generations.

Affirmative action, as Professor Mansfield sees it, can more easily be justified on grounds of retributive rather than distributive justice—that is, it functions in part as a measure of revenge for past wrongs. The principal question for Professor Mansfield concerning such programs, however, is whether they serve to build up or to tear down the personal and corporate pride of the persons they seek to serve. In his judgment, the effects are corrosive and destructive to individuals in our society as well as to the relationships among our citizens. He also believes that affirmative action violates the very principles on which our Constitution was built, in that it interferes with the right of individual consent and makes citizens dependent on government for their rights.

No decision of the Supreme Court, however, has ever adopted the proposition that the Constitution must be color-blind. Indeed, it has rejected this proposition on a number of occasions. In numerous cases, the Court has also established the constitutionality of race-conscious remedial measures. The Court has construed Title VII of the Civil Rights Act of 1964 as requiring the use of racial preferences for the purpose of hiring and advancing those who have been adversely affected by past discriminatory employment practices, *even at the expense of other employees innocent of discrimination.* (Emphasis added.) (*Franks v. Bowman Transportation Co.*, 424 U.S. 747, 767-768, 96 S.Ct. 1251, 1265-1266 [1976].) Federal regulations also clearly establish that race-conscious action is not only permitted but required to accomplish the remedial objectives of Title VI. The Supreme Court has declared that racial classifications are not *per se* invalid under the Fourteenth Amendment.

A race-conscious remedy is compelling, according to Justice Powell (in a concurring opinion in another case), when two requirements are met: First, to impose a race-conscious remedy, the governmental body must have the authority to act in response to identified discrimination; second, the governmental body must make finding demonstrating the existence of illegal discrimination. (*Fullilove v. Klutznick,* 448 U.S. 778, 100 S.Ct. 2758 [1980].) The advocates of racial classification admit that it is susceptible to misuse and that it may be justified only by showing an important purpose for its application. The remedial purposes designed by racial classification must serve important governmental objectives and must be substantially related to achievement of these objectives. The choice of remedies to redress racial discrimination is "a balancing process left, within appropriate constitutional or statutory limits, to the sound discretion of the trial court." (*Franks v. Bowman Transportation Co.,* 424 U.S. 747, 794, 96 S.Ct. 1251, 1278 [1976]. Justice Powell concurring in part and dissenting in part.)

Professor Stanley M. Johanson considers the question of racial classification in his lecture "Minority Admission Policies and Procedures: Access to the Professions." He points out that over the last three decades admission to professional schools, specifically to law schools, has become much more selective. In effect, the decision about who is admitted to the legal profession in our country is now made by the admissions committees of the law schools. This is a far different situation from the not-too-remote past, when almost anyone could gain admission to law school and the process of weeding out candidates to the profession came during law school itself or at the point of the bar examination.

This change occurred at the same time in our history as the flowering of the Civil Rights Movement. What might have been a normal influx of minority applicants into the professions was rendered problematical, since minority applicants tended to score less highly on the standardized tests that became a part of the application requirements during this same period. Professor Johanson points out that there are many minority applicants to professional schools who are capable of excellent performance both in school and in the profession, but whose credentials are marginally lower than some of those competing with them. He argues that it is, therefore, in the interest of our society as well as of the academic institutions involved that the minority status of the applicants be one of the factors taken into consideration when decisions on admission are made.

We are far from consensus on the issue of giving special preference to citizens because of their minority status. Five Justices of the Supreme Court concurred in the decision of the *Bakke* case which stated that preferring members of any group for no reason other than race or ethnic origin is discrimination for its own sake, forbidden by the Constitution. While the Court held that a class-based remedy is not permissible, it found it permissible to apply a racial classification which aids persons who are perceived as members of relatively victimized groups at the expense of other innocent individuals when there are judicial, legislative, or administrative findings of constitutional or statutory violations. This position of the Court—which made a distinction between remedial action, which is permissible, and racial preference as such, which is impermissible—met with strong dissent from those who believe, as Justice Harlan did in the case of *Plessy v. Ferguson*, that the color-blind Constitution absolutely prohibits invidious discrimination by government and that the Constitution is wholly neutral in forbidding racial discrimination, whatever the race may be of those who are its victims.

Justice Stewart, joined by Justice Renquist, in a dissenting opinion in the case of *Fullilove v. Klutznick*, stressed that the rule that under our Constitution the government may never act to the detriment of a person solely because of that person's race cannot be any different when the persons injured by a racially biased law are not members of a racial minority. The guarantee of equal protection is universal in its application to all persons without regard to any difference of race, of color, or of nationality. Consequently, stated Justice Stewart, from the perspective of a person detrimentally affected by a racially discriminatory law, "the arbitrariness and unfairness is entirely the same, whatever his skin color and whatever the law's purpose, be it purportedly 'for the promotion of the public good' or otherwise." (*Fullilove v. Klutznick*, 448 U.S. 448, 526, 100 S.Ct. 2758, 2799 [1980].)

In the *Bakke* case, Justice Marshall expressed the view that "it is more than a little ironic that, after several hundred years of class-based discrimination against Negroes, the Court is unwilling to hold that a class-based remedy for that discrimination is permissible." (438 U.S. 265, 400, 98 S.Ct. 2733, 2804 [1978].) This view is hardly convincing. A second wrong cannot turn injustice into justice. Furthermore, if racial

characteristics are to provide a relevant basis for
preferential treatment, the need would arise for a racial code with a concomitant procedure for the racial
classification of individuals. Such an idea is abhorrent
to those who value the ideals of equality and freedom.

The idea of a "melting pot" envisions a nation
where race is irrelevant. Yet in the history of the
deliberations of Congress and of the Supreme Court,
few questions have been more perplexing and
divisive than those arising from purposeful discrimination and particularly the enforcement of the post-
Civil War amendments. A democratic society strives
to be undivided by such considerations as skin
pigmentation or the origin of its citizens. Measures
that attempt to reach this goal of national unity by
means of transient political and legislative acts seldom
flower into actual and full realization of the ideals of
the Due Process and Equal Protection clauses, which
call for equal opportunity for all regardless of race or
color and for a government that governs impartially.

True national unity flourishes when the nation is
united by a shared allegiance to higher values. In my
lecture "Patriotism as a Unifying Force," I concentrate the discussion of the unifying effects of patriotism on three virtues which make patriotism distinct in
the context of our times: loyalty, readiness to defend
one's country, and tolerance. Loyalty means a fidelity
to the nation that emanates from love and devotion to
one's country. The citizen's allegiance to the State
does not always mean allegiance to a given government, since governments may use their coercive
power to oppress their own people. I try to explain
that in the United States the citizen meets the re-

quirement of loyalty by adhering to the values instilled in our institutions by our forefathers and by
preserving the rights and prerogatives of democracy.

The State's chief concern is the maintenance of
stability, justice, and most of all independence. Its
citizens have a reciprocal obligation to bear arms in
the country's defense. The safety of our nation is valuable not only to the United States but also to the freedom of the world. Aggression is an act of infamy. Defense against aggression is an act of patriotism. A
citizen's duty to his country and his fellow citizens
makes readiness to defend his nation and sacrifice
himself a virtue we must live up to in order to deserve
the name of patriot.

The unity that patriotism seeks to build does not
call for conformity of belief and expression. Our freedom will be lost if all of us are compelled to think,
feel, and act in consonance with patterns dictated by
those who see treason in dissidence and use patriotism as a club to attack fellow citizens who refuse to
accept dominance over their minds. Tolerance of dissenting views and free exchange of ideas provide the
atmosphere in which freedom can live and grow.

The ideals of a democratic society call for placing all
citizens, regardless of race, into the mainstream of
American life. This can be accomplished only by
educational and cultural endeavors that enhance a
faith in the dignity and worth of every individual. By
changing the hearts of individuals, we transform
society. We should seek to effect such changes by in-
sisting that the proposition that a free society is based
on the dignity of every human being is founded not
only on the revealed word of God but on reason itself.

DEMOGRAPHICS, DEMOCRACY, AND EDUCATION

by

Robert L. Payton

Robert L. Payton

Robert L. Payton was appointed president of Exxon Education Foundation March 1, 1977. He had earlier served as president of Hofstra University and C.W. Post College, and was U.S. Ambassador to the Federal Republic of Cameroon from 1967-69.

Mr. Payton was on the staff of Washington University in St. Louis for nine years, serving as vice chancellor from 1961-66. His earlier career included editorships of a weekly newspaper and a trade magazine. During World War II he served with the 11th Airborne Division.

Educated at the University of Chicago, from which he holds a master's degree, Mr. Payton was awarded an honorary doctor of literature degree by Adelphi University in 1975. He is also a commander of the Order of the Bamoun Spider and officier of the Order of Valor of the United Republic of Cameroon. In July 1984 he received the award for Distinguished Service to Higher Education from the Council for Advancement and Support of Education.

Mr. Payton is chairman of the Columbia Seminar on Philanthropy and of the Research Committee of Independent Sector. He is a member of the board of the Institute of International Education, the Council of American Ambassadors, the International Council for Educational Development, Technoserve, the Council for Advancement and Support of Education, and Independent Sector.

DEMOGRAPHICS, DEMOCRACY, AND EDUCATION

by

Robert L. Payton

There are important changes taking place in American society. We do not face simply the now-familiar syndrome of "future shock" generated by technology and information coming faster than we can handle or absorb it. Nor is it any longer a matter of popular culture imposing constant new challenges to our sensibilities.

The changes of which I speak are demographic, and they reveal the emerging reshaping of American society. The first set of facts is transitory: The Baby Boom of the period from 1946 to 1962 is passing through, and for a very long time we will live in a society that is disproportionately old after decades of being unusually youthful.

The second set of facts is permanent: The ethnic profile of the United States is changing dramatically, and that change will continue. The United States we have known will not be what it was during its first two centuries. We are entering a period of being less *Western* in our ethnic and cultural makeup. The questions that arise from such changes will force us to think more carefully about the Western values that should be preserved.

I

On the demographic changes, let me use the recent excellent study, *All One System*, compiled and written by Harold L. Hodgkinson and published just a few months ago by the Institute for Educational Leadership. Hodgkinson groups his information into five categories: Births, Age, Family Status, Regions, and Education. (I should point out that Hodgkinson is aware of the limitations of his discipline. He first quotes Kenneth Boulding in saying that " 'of all the social sciences, demographics is most like the science of celestial mechanics'—we look for the huge unseen engines that make social systems work in certain ways.")

1. *Births.* ". . . some groups have a lot more children than others." A group needs a rate of 2.1 children per female to stay even; that is the fertility level of Puerto Rican women in the U.S. at present. Cubans are at 1.3, however, and whites are at 1.7, while blacks are at 2.4, and Mexican-Americans at 2.9.

2. *Age.* Differential rates of fertility result in the swelling and contracting of age groups up the bar graphs used to measure such things. The average white American is 31, the average black is 25, the average Hispanic but 22. Such age groupings or cohorts show up in school enrollments: Six states (including California and Texas) now have 35 percent or more minority enrollments, and eleven (including New York, Florida, and Illinois) have between 25 and 35 percent.

3. *Family Status.* "In 1955," Hodgkinson writes, "60% of the households in the U.S. consisted of a working father, housewife mother, and two or more school age children. In 1980, that family unit was only 11% of our homes, and in 1985 it is 7%, an astonishing change." Hodgkinson makes a further point:

"The Census tells us that 59% of the children born in 1983 will live with only one parent before reaching age 18—this now becomes the NORMAL childhood experience. Of every 100 children born today:
- 12 will be born out of wedlock
- 40 will be born to parents who will divorce before the child is 18
- 5 will be born to parents who separate
- 2 will be born to parents of whom one will die before the child reaches 18
- 41 will reach age 18 'normally'."

4. *Regions.* The nation will, despite the shift to the sun belt and other phenomena, remain "eastern-oriented"—that is, 80% of the population will live in the Eastern and Central time zones, and only 20% will live in the Mountain and Pacific time zones, at least through the year 2000.

5. *Education.* The bulk of Hodgkinson's paper is about the consequences for education of these demographic changes. He points out that there is a perceptual change in the way he is trying to look at education here. Rather than talking in terms of elementary and secondary schools and four-year under-

graduate colleges, he is defining the school in terms of *the people who are moving through it.* Here are some of the educational consequences of the demographic changes:

> More children entering school from poverty households
>
> More children entering school from single-parent households
>
> More children from minority backgrounds
>
> More "latch-key" children
>
> Fewer white middle-class, suburban children

Hodgkinson gave me a further revealing fact: there are now more Muslims than Episcopalians in the United States. (After learning that, I happened to look at the religious affiliations of the members of Congress: there are 67 Episcopalians, and no Muslims.) Immigrants and refugees are arriving in the United States in the largest numbers in fifty years. For the first time in our history, most of the new arrivals are non-European.

My first point is that there are major demographic changes taking place in the United States. Some of these changes are ethnic in character. As Milton Gordon of the University of Massachusetts has suggested, the Anglo-European dominance of American society may begin to give way to other influences.

My second point will be that these changes are not unique to the United States. The examples I will cite include France, the Soviet Union, the world of Islam, and the African nation of Cameroon.

II

A. *France*

You may have read that the weekly magazine *Le Figaro* (a rough journalistic equivalent to *Life* and the *Saturday Evening Post*) has published a demographic analysis of France carrying the title "Will We Still Be French in 30 Years?" The point of the article—at least in the words of the magazine's editor—is that dramatic changes are taking place in France that must be talked about openly and candidly. The changes are in the demographic profile of France itself. The editor says that the foreign-born population now on French soil is largely of Mediterranean and African origin and is 90 percent Islamic in culture and religion.

The authors of the article and the editors of the journal have been denounced by members of the French cabinet as being racist in intent, and the article as being statistically insupportable in any event. The rates of change have been deliberately exaggerated, these voices say, and other factors, especially poverty and lack of education, are minimized or ignored. The political character of the debate is heightened by the rapid rise to public prominence of Jacques Le Pen, leader of the party called the National Front. Le Pen, a rightist with many qualities reminiscent of the chauvinism of the 1930s, says that France's two most serious problems are crime and immigration—and that the two are related.

Flora Lewis, the *New York Times* European correspondent, has been writing frequently about this new phenomenon in France and elsewhere; one recent article of hers was entitled "Race Issues in Europe."

Lewis's point is that France and Britain are entering a period of disruptive social change—disruptive largely because of their relative inexperience in dealing with ethnic groups within. "Racism," she writes, "which many Europeans thought was a peculiar fault of Americans, has developed in countries that believed they were above it without noticing that they took national identity as one race for granted." American success in dealing with racial tension is now being looked to by Europeans as a guide to solving Europe's problems.

B. *The Soviet Union*

The Soviet Union faces a more aggravated version of the same phenomenon that Hodgkinson has described in the U.S. The case of the USSR is of interest to us for several reasons. The United States and the Soviet Union are vast in size, rich in natural resources, and demographically complex. Each is also offered to the world as a model of a philosophy of government.

A recent study published by the Council on Foreign Relations points out that although the 137 million Russians remain by far the largest group in Soviet society, they represent a bare majority. The most rapid growth and continuing high birth rates are to be found among the Muslims of Central Asia, who now constitute 17 percent of the population. There is even further complexity. There are more than a hundred nationalities in the Soviet Union, and most of them still occupy lands that link them directly to a long and—for them, at least—distinguished and honorable history. There are twenty-one nationalities in the Soviet Union that number more than a million people, and nineteen of those "speak mainly their mother tongue."

Different societies respond differently to the changes brought about by culture in confrontation with the values of modernization. That problem seems to have been solved by force in the Soviet Union, especially during its early years when it imposed collectivization and industrialization on an underdeveloped agricultural society.

C. *Islam*

The recent experience of Iran provides the textbook example of an effort to reverse the movement of modernization. The values of culture are seen to override the values of economics. Bernard Lewis, in a brief but illuminating essay in the *Washington Quarterly*, traces the course of the rise of Islamic fundamentalism. To understand the phenomenon of Islamic fundamentalism, Lewis says, there are five points to be gleaned from its view of the world and its recent history. The first is "a total interpenetration of religion and politics" in Islam. The second is that for many decades there has been a mood of disillusion in the Islamic world as it watched the growing power and influence of the West. The third point is the turnaround that began with the oil crisis little more than a decade ago; the new importance of the Islamic world growing out of that crisis resulted in a "feeling of power and exultation" among Muslims the world over. Lewis's fourth point is that the Iranian revolution led by the Ayatollah Khomeini is a real revolution, having consequences as important for the world as did the French and Russian revolutions. The fifth and final observation is that Islamic fundamentalism began by rejecting Western influences and purging them in favor of a purer and simpler model of Islamic life. That fervor has now turned from external enemies toward internal ones: ". . . what matters," Lewis paraphrases, "is not imperialism and zionism and foreign invasion, and so on, but rather the corruption of our own society, the impiety of our rulers . . . [those] who have destroyed Islam from within."

I have included the changes under way in the Islamic world to emphasize the fact that ethnic considerations ignore national boundaries. Ethnic considerations, carried to extremes, as we have seen, put forward a different social and institutional order.

D. *The United Republic of Cameroon*

Cameroon is an artifact of history. Its people are ethnically diverse. They are, to use outmoded but convenient anthropological categories, a mixture of Bantu peoples who have migrated up from central and south Africa, and Sudanese people who migrated or were driven by slave traders from northwest Africa. Cameroon is divided religiously into a Christian segment in the south and a Muslim segment in the north, with undetermined numbers of people still following indigenous religious practices and beliefs. The large eastern section of the country is French-speaking and the smaller western part of the country is English-speaking—but there are about 60 African languages spoken in this nation of less than ten million people who represent some 125 definable ethnic groups or tribes.

Cameroon is a word derived from the Portuguese, and so the new nation owes even its name to Europeans—in this case to slave traders who travelled the west African coast in the sixteenth century. In the late nineteenth century the Germans won a race from the English to colonize the territory, but England and France took over from the Germans after the First World War. A generation grew up under a mandate of the League of Nations and a second generation grew up under a trusteeship of the United Nations. Cameroon won its independence in 1960. The French-speaking eastern part then united with the English-speaking western part and in 1961 Cameroon became a federal republic. The two states of the Cameroon Federal Republic were merged into the United Republic of Cameroon in 1970.

Cameroon is one of Africa's few success stories. Apart from some political unrest and an early rebellion, and in spite of occasional external interference from its Marxist neighbor to the south, Cameroon has been an island of relative stability in a sea of discord and disorder. To study its quarter-century of independence is to study a miracle of ethnic politics at its most effective. While all the ethnic forces in Cameroon work to pull it apart, effective political leadership and management have pulled it together into a state. It has held together long enough, it appears, to have persuaded many people in all parts of the country to realize that the tensions of living in a multicultural society are better than the alternative of violence that accompanies ethnic conflict and social disorder.

There are some who don't accept that analysis, of course. There are some who would prefer to have two Cameroons, or five, or at least to have autonomy for their own ancestral home. However, the fervent nationalism of the past century or more has been based on the conviction that the state is more important by far than any of the discrete ethnic or political elements within it. It is this conviction that has guided the emergence of Cameroon. But it is also a similar conviction that has sustained Nigeria in crushing—at terrible human cost—the effort of Biafra to secede.

III

The tension between ethnic group and state is the tie that binds the experience of Cameroon to that of the Soviet Union. In a different form, it is the tension that now threatens not the state but French peace of mind. The presence of new and powerful cultural forces within France may change what it means to say that one is "French." For Islamic fundamentalists, there is but one faith and it is coextensive with the state.

What does the new ethnic profile hold out for us? Will the American experience continue to be the beacon for the world? It is reasonable to assume that rapid rates of change—demographic, ethnic, cultural—will test our cohesiveness and that of many other societies in the decades ahead. Such changes in our society as well as others have often resulted in ethnic conflict. We have been spared some of the worst consequences of ethnic conflict, in spite of our great ethnic diversity. Much of the rest of the world seems bent on self-destruction by ethnic conflict—as Donald Horowitz has written in his major study of *Ethnic Groups in Conflict,* "Ethnicity is at the center of politics in country after country, a potent source of challenges to the cohesion of states and of international tension." He then offers this list of connections: "Biafra, Bangladesh, and Burundi, Beirut, Brussels, and Belfast."

Our Anglo-European traditions offer us little comfort. In addition to Brussels and Belfast there are two dozen other persistent centers of ethnic conflict in western Europe.

Michael Walzer, in *Spheres of Justice,* identified *membership in a human community* as the most important social good. The ways that we permit entry into membership in our own national community express a judgment of ourselves as well as of others who would join us. Our history is a record of efforts to keep ethnic identity subordinate to national identity—and that is exactly the same challenge that faces the Soviet Union on the one hand and Cameroon on the other.

My purpose in discussing this topic is to suggest its importance not just to our society in some large but unspecified political sense, but to our educational system in particular. At one very practical level, the ethnic question reflects concern about bilingualism in instruction; at another very practical level the concern is about the increasingly familiar phenomenon of teachers with different cultural backgrounds from their students, and students with different cultural backgrounds from one another.

In Sullivan High School in Chicago, to illustrate the language problem, there are said to be forty-five first languages spoken other than English.

To illustrate the larger educational problem, one merely needs to ask oneself, as I have frequently done as I have tried to consider the ideal of "liberal education": Is it really universally applicable—even within the United States—or is it simply "Eurocentric"?

What is often called *civic education*—the education of the citizen—becomes a particularly important issue for us *now*, as we educate the teachers who will educate the children who will grow up in a different America. The tradition we pass on, neither as successful nor as romantic as we often pretend that it is, is of an America that is the world's most successful multicultural society, the highest achievement of ethnic accommodation and toleration in history.

If we are to remain a free and open and democratic society, then we must better understand the elements of our tradition that have made that possible. We inherited that tradition, after all; we have modified it, extended it, and broadcast it to the world, but we did not invent it.

The test, as always, is whether we will pass the tradition on, stronger and more unifying than when we received it.

OUR CONSTITUTION: WILL IT SURVIVE ANOTHER 200 YEARS?

by

Daniel K. Inouye

Daniel K. Inouye

Daniel K. Inouye is the senior United States Senator from the state of Hawaii. He was elected to the Hawaiian Territorial House of Representatives in 1954 and served as Majority Leader from 1954 to 1958, then in 1958 was elected to the Territorial Senate. In 1959 he became the first U.S. Congressman from the state of Hawaii. He was elected to the U.S. Senate in 1962, and as Secretary of the Democratic Conference has been third-ranking leader among Senate Democrats since 1978.

In the Senate, Senator Inouye has sat on the Appropriations Committee since 1971. He is the Ranking Democrat on the Subcommittee on Foreign Operations. He also serves on the Commerce, Science, and Transportation Committee and is Ranking Democrat of the Subcommittee on Merchant Marine.

Among his other commitments to public service, Senator Inouye was Senior Counsellor to the National Bipartisan Commission on Central America and Chairman of the Senate Democratic Central America Study Group. He was also the Senate Democrat representative to the White House-Congressional bipartisan deficit reduction group in 1984. That year he served as the Co-Chairman of the Democratic National Convention. Earlier he had served as Chairman of the Rules Committee for the 1980 Convention and Keynote Speaker for the 1968 Convention. He was honored with the Splendid American Award from the Thomas A. Dooley Foundation in 1967, with the National Intelligence Distinguished Service Medal in 1978, and the Admiral of the Ocean Sea Award in 1980.

Senator Inouye received his B.A. from the University of Hawaii and his J.D. from the George Washington Law School. He enlisted in the U.S. Army in March 1943 at age 18, served with the 442nd Infantry Regimental Combat Team in Europe, received a battlefield commission in November 1944, and was wounded in April 1945. He was decorated with the Distinguished Service Cross, the Bronze Star, and the Purple Heart with cluster. His autobiography, Journey to Washington, was published in 1967.

OUR CONSTITUTION: WILL IT SURVIVE ANOTHER 200 YEARS?

by

Senator Daniel K. Inouye

I

James Madison warned in the tenth *Federalist* paper that the principal threat to our, or any other, democracy was the establishment of a "faction" composed of a majority of its citizens. And as Madison prophesied, threats to our Constitution have, in fact, been most real when groups "united by common impulse of passion, or of interests, adverse to the rights of other citizens, or the permanent aggregate interests of the community" have attempted to impose their visions or interests upon our nation. Either by wisdom or by force, our Constitution and our freedoms have been preserved because no single and exclusive vision of America has been able to prevail. Instead, a diverse people, joined by threads of freedom and opportunity, have been able to survive and flourish.

In the future, however, we may be forced to confront "factions" which the breadth and diversity of our nation will not be able to overcome. I fear this will occur if America succumbs to the temptation to develop and pursue policies which fail to accommodate the racial and cultural evolution which is already taking place in our nation. The resolution of factional challenges has, in America, always been made in the context of a nation whose heritage was essentially European and Caucasian. There has never been any real or perceived threat to the fact that we are fundamentally a white nation. However, the demographics of recent years suggest that this picture may someday change and the tinges of fear in anticipation of this fundamental change are already being felt. The manner in which we address this apparently inevitable evolution may well determine whether our form of government will survive. For if, as may well be the case, racial and cultural divisions are exacerbated by policies which create a distinct underclass, permanent and irreconcilable factions entirely indifferent to the "aggregate interests" of our nation may ultimately prevail.

America is not, at this point, "threatened" by a nonwhite majority. However, there is no denying that the day may come when the influence and sheer numbers of today's "minorities" will either redefine or fundamentally divide much of our nation. Today, minorities comprise 14 percent of our nation's population. Within the next one hundred years this proportion is expected to rise until in the year 2080 they comprise over 25 percent of all Americans. Thereafter the proportion of nonwhite Americans will continue to increase—in fact the Census Bureau anticipates that the total number of white citizens in our country is expected to begin to decrease shortly after the turn of this century. An America with a nonwhite majority might fairly be anticipated when we celebrate the quadricentennial of our Constitution.

Other trends in our racial makeup will be more immediately felt. By the turn of the century, those of Hispanic origin can be anticipated to constitute the single largest ethnic minority in the United States. By that time 30 percent of all Americans between the ages of eighteen and twenty-four will be from a minority. And today's cities are increasingly controlled by other than whites—over 250 cities are currently governed by black mayors, a quadrupling over the last twenty years.

It is foreseeable, and perhaps inevitable, that the day will come when our nation will no longer be an Anglo-American culture tolerating and accommodating pockets of minorities. Rather we will have become a nation of minorities. If this comes to pass, the question that must be addressed is whether our government and culture will grow and flourish or whether we will become a nation of intractable factions with little in common except fear and the desire to dominate.

II

Our current response to this distant but apparent horizon is far from heartening. In response to encroaching "foreign" cultures, many in power appear to be issuing an often desperate cry for homogeneity. Social and economic divisions which mirror racial borders are increasingly treated as inevitable. We are told that race and culture should be treated as irrelevant to success while in fact the forces and prejudices of the existing "market" contribute to the establishment of permanent colored underclasses which may someday outnumber those who control the "market." In many ways there appears to be a retrenchment manifested by the declaration and imposition of a largely mythological and artificial vision of America's culture and economy. Perhaps this attempt is born of a desire to preserve and make permanent this vision before it is "too late"; perhaps it is an attempt to exclude access in the absence of trust in the result which genuine openness and opportunity would yield.

In small and subtle ways Madison's feared faction of the majority may be currently coming to pass, willing to limit freedom because of fear that another majority may someday control. In 1983, the Senate Committee on the Judiciary made the following statement in its report accompanying the Senate Immigration Reform Bill.

"No one seeking to enter the United States should be discriminated against because of race, color, or religion as has sometimes happened in the past. This nation does have a right, however, to expect that anyone wishing the freedom and opportunity which is to be found in America . . . will seek to assimilate into American society, adopting and supporting the public values, beliefs, and customs underlying America's success."

Our Constitution makes no mention of assimilation

and support of American culture and beliefs as a precondition of freedom and opportunity for either immigrants or citizens. The institutional imposition of such a requirement does not bode well for any who might be considered "foreign."

The same report subsequently restated its commitment to cultural homogeneity.

> "Pluralism, within a united American nation, has been the single greatest strength of this country. This unity comes from a common language and a core public culture of certain shared values, beliefs, and customs which make us distinctly 'Americans.' "

There should be no need to cry for strength where strength and confidence exist. I am concerned that such expressions are more a reflection of fear of the foreign than a proud claim of success. And the appeal of this fear, shrouded in chauvinism, seems increasingly prevalent.

The current passion for school prayer is often accompanied by arguments that it is justified because we are a "Christian nation." There is a tone of desperation in this willful disregard of our nation's commitment to religious freedom. Yet such passionate cries are spoken by responsible leaders who appeal to a vision of an America made great by God and now dissolving into confusion and unbelief. I wonder how well, and for how long, our freedoms might withstand even such implicit chauvinism in a nation increasingly other than that envisioned in the American dream?

III

Any divisions created by rhetoric or prejudice might be without significance if economic integration were genuinely available to those who might otherwise be treated as separate. But either by accident or by design, little is being done in this regard.

Education is properly viewed as an avenue to mobility and integration. But current trends in this regard suggest only a painful future. If high-school graduation rates are used as a measure of educational success, the fact that 38.8 percent of Hispanic youths and 22 percent of black youths dropped out of high school last year hardly suggests the creation of the kind of nation where learning and the possession of the most basic academic skills will serve as a point of cohesion. Even among minority students who stay in school, statistics available from those states which require "competency testing" prior to graduation suggest that a division is present and growing. In Florida, for example, 95 percent of the white students passed the minimum-competency test on their first try; only 35 percent of the black students did so. If the development of leadership and models of success via higher education is looked to, the figures and trends are no more hopeful. Excluding Asians, minorities constitute 20 percent of the nation's college-age population, but they account for only 8 percent of the Ph.D.'s awarded, and 5.8 percent of the M.A.'s. Their rate of entrance into medical school and law school has actually decreased in the last five years and, with sources of federal and state financial aid being diminished, can be expected to further decrease. And on the most basic of levels, that of literacy, the further division of our nation only worsens, based upon the absence of opportunity and an alienation from even the slightest possibility of access. Some experts suggest that functional illiteracy, that is, an inability to read at the fifth-grade level and to compute the most basic of math problems, may be as high as 40 percent among minority youth. It is predicted to be at the 56-percent level among adult Hispanics and 44 percent among adult blacks. In contrast, only 16 percent of adult whites fall into this unfortunate category.

Even the most casual of observers cannot help but note that these figures reflect the seeds of a nation divided along social and economic lines that almost precisely mirror race and culture. Yet our current response is to simply hide behind a rhetoric of equality and "Americanism," as public education is denigrated by those who encourage tax credits to individuals who can afford to flee to private schools, as more "discipline" is offered as a superior solution to the development of improved schools by way of a commitment of financial resources, and as the spectre of "cheaters" is used to justify the reduction of funds available to provide loans for students seeking a college education.

To provide more specific examples with regard to programs which impact the education of minorities—in the last five years the current administration has proposed a 25-percent reduction in federal funding for compensatory education for the disadvantaged; a 31-percent reduction in funds available for bilingual education; the elimination of the Indian education program; a $230-million reduction in elementary and secondary education block grants together with the elimination of programs for special populations; and the elimination of 100,000 student grants and $103 million in guaranteed student loans.

By such policies we invite and perhaps fuel the formation of a nation within a nation which, without hope or opportunity, can only care nothing for the "aggregate interest" of which they are not a part. Can our, or any, democratic constitution survive such divisions? Can it survive the choice to leave entire classes of citizens without even the most elementary tool for success?

IV

Failures with regard to education may only ensure the continuation of economic divisions which currently exist. The percentage of blacks who are poor—33.8 percent—is triple the rate for whites. Black unemployment is 15 percent or 2.3 times the white rate; the Hispanic rate is 11.2, "only" double that of whites. And perhaps most worrisome for the future, teenage unemployment stands at 44 percent for blacks and 11.2 percent for Hispanics.

Among minorities who are employed, a disproportionately high number hold low-status jobs. Blacks are underrepresented in professional and technical occupations by 70 percent and Hispanics are underrepresented by 50 percent. All of this represents trends and figures which are the worst in recent history. The vaunted economic recovery fueled by a reliance on the market has done nothing for our nation's minorities. In fact the only substantial group to have statistically benefited by the recovery is white males.

Participation in the middle class has been viewed since the time of Aristotle as a key to the stability of a democracy. Yet for the first time in recent history, access to the middle class in this country is increasingly foreclosed as the middle class actually shrinks as a portion of the total division of income.

Again, our government's response to these realities of ultimate division has been far from hopeful. Virtually all programs and policies aimed at economic integration have been reduced or attacked. Minority set-asides have been eliminated or reduced; the job corps and other youth training programs are targets for elimination; government affirmative-action programs have been placed on the administration's chopping block; and the government has joined in attacks on private affirmative-action programs which have been voluntarily entered into or which have been mandated by law. In their place has been offered the "subminimum wage," the promise of the marketplace, and the rhetoric of absolute equality.

The rhetoric of absolute equality appears, in fact, to be one of the more appealing elements of an emerging "American" perspective of indifference to real economic and racial divisions. The rhetoric is, essentially, that the law should recognize no racial accommodations at all. However, in application it is used to defend an unwillingness to request or enforce any recognition of race in the framing of remedies to address prior racist policies or the realities of inherent economic disadvantage. Opportunity is not available on an equal basis to all in a system historically constructed and maintained to limit opportunities or enforce segregation. And to now pretend that equality of opportunity means only to treat everyone as though they were born to the same advantage serves only to further demean those individuals and peoples who have no chance to enter the contest on an equal footing.

More than one hundred and fifty years ago Jefferson recognized that the market provided no answer to the social and moral dilemmas facing a nation. "Merchants," he wrote, "have no country. The mere spot they stand on does not constitute so strong an attachment as that from which they draw their gains." How long can our Constitution survive a policy that permits the division of our nation along economic and racial lines? Or, a policy that leaves economic and social equality in the hands of the Jeffersonian "merchants"?

V

One avenue for employment that the government has provided is the armed services. After the war in Vietnam, we did away with the draft and instituted an all-volunteer army. Although the Department of Defense has officially indicated that it is pleased with the demographics and educational background of its recruits, available figures show that a disproportionate number of minority members are currently serving and that an exceedingly low number of college graduates have volunteered.

Approximately 25 percent of our armed forces are black. And while the recent recession has led to an increase in nonminority white recruits, the long-term trend is for an ever-increasing population of minority recruits. At least one eminent sociologist believes that there could come a point in the relatively near future when virtually all of our soldiers will be black. He attributes this to a "tripping effect" whereby as the proportion of minorities grows, whites will become less likely to enlist and somewhere along the line the disproportion will become so profound that enlistment will no longer be a viable option for whites, thereby leaving a solid minority army.

The social and political implications of a minority army defending a country controlled by a separate, largely white, class are staggering. And while this may never come to pass, it is certainly worth considering in terms of the strength of our nation and stability of our government. Even if this worst case does not come to pass, it is clear that the military is not the same as it was during World War I or World War II. The services are confronted with problems related to race and ethnicity that have not really existed prior to this period in time. The manner in which these problems are addressed may well influence the attitudes and beliefs of millions of future soldiers and veterans as to who fights and dies for his country, and who may hide behind a shield of relative economic security. What impact will these developments have on the survival of our nation and Constitution?

VI

When our founding fathers drafted our Constitution, we had a vast land mass to our west populated by Native Americans who posed no real threat to our na-

tional security. To our east the Atlantic Ocean
provided a virtually impenetrable barrier. Any threats
from the north and south were marginal. But today, in
an age of ICBMs and nuclear submarines, the threats
to our immediate security are most genuine and we
now spend approximately $300 billion a year to assure
our defense. One of the results of increased defense
spending, coupled with the president's tax cuts of
1981, has been a current deficit projected to exceed
$200 billion. The implications of this deficit, and the
steps that have been proposed to reduce it, are both
real and disturbing with regard to the possibility of
establishing genuine racial equality.

The Congress is currently debating the so-called
Gramm-Rudman-Hollings Deficit Reduction Pro-
posal. Under the terms of this draconian measure,
spending cuts would be mandated in order to meet
identified deficit levels. Even the briefest examination of where these cuts are likely to fall does not bode
well for the already deepening division between rich
and poor—between those who have and the largely
have-not nonwhite underclass. A brief list of cuts
which would disproportionately affect minorities include: reducing the Food Stamp Program by $500
million, cutting the Pell Grant Program by $215 mil-
lion, and reducing federal grants to assist educational-
ly deprived children by $174 million. The Head Start
Program would be cut by $50 million, vocational edu-
cation grants reduced by $42 million, summer youth
employment by $162 million, and the Work Incentive
Program by $11.4 million. Child Welfare Services
would lose $26 million, Community Services block

grants $15 million, fuel assistance to low income $97.4 million, and $50 million from the School Nutrition and Lunch Programs.

In the event that Congress does not possess the political "courage" to impose such cuts, the president will be permitted effectively to mandate them—a desperate legislative provision which in itself threatens the balance of power established in our Constitution. Pursuant to such a plan, it is not difficult to see who will have to be sacrificed for our tax breaks and defense buildup.

But what price will our children, and our form of government ultimately have to pay for a foundation established on the basis of such choices?

VII

The right to vote, and thereby participate in the governance of our nation, has always served as a factor which mitigated the impact of factions. But here too, there may be a price to be paid for current policies. Our Voting Rights Acts have ensured the right of all citizens to participate in elections. Yet black participation in elections remains approximately 10 percent below whites on a proportional basis. Hispanic voter participation is approximately 5 percent lower than whites. In total, only approximately 43 percent of eligible blacks and 48 percent of eligible Hispanics are likely to take advantage of their right to vote. While many factors contribute to these disturbing statistics, a principal element identified by experts is the poor quality of education generally available to these populations. Providing the opportunity to vote means nothing without a basic understanding of the significance—and content—of a ballot.

With regard to those who do exercise their franchise, as minorities continue to grow in number and political power, the continuance of a current trend may present an even more significant problem. One of the things made clear by the most recent presidential election is the deepening of a split between white and minority voters. President Reagan piled up 63 percent of the white vote, and in some southern states far heftier margins. Walter Mondale attracted nearly 90 percent of the increased numbers of black voters. Increasingly, national and local elections are similarly divisible simply along racial and economic lines.

I do not think that our founding fathers desired racially divided elections or an educational system which effectively deprives many of the franchise. Will our Constitution survive another two hundred years of such development?

VIII

I am not wise enough to chart a course which will assure the survival of our Constitution for the next two hundred years. I know, however, that the path to survival lies in remaking a choice originally framed by Thomas Jefferson:

> "Men are . . . naturally divided into two parties: 1) Those who fear and distrust the people, and wish to draw all powers from them into the hands of higher classes. 2) Those who identify

themselves with the people, have confidence in
them, cherish and consider them as the most honest and safe . . . depository of the public interest."

Long ago America chose to "cherish and consider" *all*
of its people as the best and only reliable "depository
of the public interest," and we have been richly
rewarded.

Ours is a nation blessed with a bountiful land—rich
in resources, in beauty, and in size—powerful enough
to adopt a belief in freedom which welcomed men and
women from all continents. The fruit of this faith has
been to increase our vigor and wealth as new ideas,
cultures, and energies have been incorporated among
our resources. Our invitation to all who cherish freedom has yielded great Americans from once feared
"minorities": President John F. Kennedy, an Irish
Catholic; Jews such as Israel Baline, who wrote "God
Bless America," and Albert Einstein; Governor
Cuomo and Lee Iaccoca from among the Italians;
Martin Luther King, George Washington Carver, and
the beginning of a roll call of honored blacks; Seiji
Ozawa and I.M. Pei, Asians among our nation's musi-
cal and architectural geniuses.

Today's minorities, blacks, Hispanics, Asians, and
other newly arrived or historically alienated groups,
continue to represent a pool from which we might
draw even greater strength. And they will do so unless we persist in treating them as a mass to be feared
or ignored. For from among them can come our
Nobel laureates, business leaders, great musicians,
wise scholars, and perhaps even presidents who can
help continue to revitalize and strengthen our nation.

As with our commitment to freedom of speech, a genuine commitment to opportunity for all might, despite considerable cost, yield a generous bounty. Despite the misgivings of some, and the genuine social tensions created, we do not burn books. Similarly, despite the costs, and the fears of some, we could only be strengthened by our decision not to relegate whole classes of human beings to an economic and educational scrap heap. I pray that we will not.

No other country on this planet would have given me the privilege of standing before you as a member of our highest legislative body. America gave me the opportunity to study, to learn, and to serve our nation. I know that racial distinctions and cultural differences need not yield to Madison's irreconcilable "factions" if opportunities are presented, rather than doors closed. And I pray that America's commitment to the value of each individual will require it to respond in a fashion that not only will permit our Constitution to survive, but will justify the great pride that all of us feel in being Americans.

EQUALITY IN AMERICA: DEMOCRACY'S CHALLENGE

by

John Hope Franklin

John Hope Franklin

John Hope Franklin is the James B. Duke Professor of History at Duke University. He is a native of Oklahoma and a graduate of Fisk University. He received the A.M. and Ph.D. degrees in history from Harvard University. He has taught at a number of institutions, including Fisk University, North Carolina Central University, and Howard University. In 1956 he went to Brooklyn College as Chairman of the Department of History there; and in 1964 he joined the faculty of the University of Chicago, and served as Chairman of the Department of History from 1967 to 1970. He was the John Matthews Manly Distinguished Service Professor from 1969 to 1982, when he became Emeritus Professor there.

Professor Franklin has written a number of books, including The Emancipation Proclamation, The Free Negro in North Carolina, Reconstruction After the Civil War, *and* A Southern Odyssey: Travelers in the Antebellum North. *Perhaps his best known book is* From Slavery to Freedom. A History of Negro Americans, *the fifth edition of which appeared in 1980.*

For many years he served on the editorial board of the Journal of Negro History. *He has served as President of the following organizations: The American Studies Association (1967), The Southern Historical Association (1970), the United Chapters of Phi Beta Kappa (1973-76), the Organization of American Historians (1975), and the American Historical Association (1979). Professor Franklin has served on many national commissions and delegations, including the National Council on the Humanities. In September and October, 1980, he was a United States delegate to the 21st General Conference of UNESCO.*

In 1978, the year he was elected to the Oklahoma Hall of Fame, he was also one of eight Americans cited by Who's Who in America *for significant contributions to society. He has been a recipient of honorary degrees from a large number of colleges and universities.*

EQUALITY IN AMERICA:
DEMOCRACY'S CHALLENGE

by

John Hope Franklin

Among the peoples of the world, those who inhabit the United States have had as much to say about equality as any. Indeed, the stated commitment to equality is as old as the nation itself. When he wrote those immortal words, "We hold these truths to be self-evident, that all men are created equal," Thomas Jefferson made the most sublime expression of equality that anyone in the Western world has ever made. It was followed by similar professions and expressions of the ideal, which became an integral part of the heritage of this country. It would be repeated by the abolitionists, by the fighters for freedom and union during the Civil War, by the Radicals during Reconstruction, and by many others in the late nineteenth century and in this century. And inherent in the dream of equality was the dream of the equal opportunity to fight for one's country, to secure an education, to obtain a job and housing, to enjoy equal protection of the laws, and to live out one's life secure in one's person and property.

In our own history, the choices we have made have usually been determined by our sense of priorities as well as by our convictions. As we fought for our independence from Britain, for example, we concluded that it was better to secure our independence *first* before doing anything about the remarkably obvious contradiction of fighting for political freedom while sternly maintaining human bondage. Thus, the fledgling United States postponed the vital question of freedom and equality at precisely the most opportune moment, when freedom and equality had the best chance of full realization. Never again—not even during the Civil War or during the great wars of the twentieth century—would ideology and objective be so congenial to each other. It was an opportunity tragically missed which, incidentally, most of the other New World colonies did not miss as they fought for and achieved independence and freedom for all.

Even when emancipation came, in the wake of the Civil War, most Americans preferred to postpone the disposition of the matter of equality until some later date, lest the mere raising of the question should exacerbate sectional and race relations and thus endanger the industrial and commercial expansion to which they eagerly looked forward. Even in our own time there have been those who have argued that when the drive for equality created inconvenience as well as resistance, prudence cautioned against "pressing too hard."

It was the lack of conviction, however, even more than the curiously distorted sense of priorities that, in the early days of the Republic, rendered so utterly difficult the achievement of anything resembling equality of opportunity. Even before the slaveholders and their allies developed a veritable theology of inequality in their proslavery arguments, white Americans did not believe in racial equality. Surely the

Founding Fathers did not. Despite what he wrote in the Declaration of Independence, Thomas Jefferson did not believe in equality; and even after he examined the ingenious work of the black astronomer, Benjamin Banneker, he continued to doubt that blacks could be the intellectual equals of whites. But there would come a time when many Americans would castigate the ambivalent Jefferson for having even *suggested* the equality of all men in the Declaration of Independence. In the 1830s Dr. Thomas Cooper, South Carolina's preeminent intellectual, led a large group of distinguished Americans in declaring that the very notion of suggesting all men are equal was not only extremely absurd but thoroughly reprehensible as well.

Meanwhile, George Fitzhugh, Virginia's outstanding social scientist, and his followers made up in zeal what they lacked in logic when they argued that the only way to have a successful social order was to base it firmly on the essential *inequality* of mankind. Some human beings, Fitzhugh argued, should be forced to perform the drudgery of life, while the work of others would lead to "progress, civilization, and refinement." Much better it be Negroes than whites who should perform this drudgery.

> "The temptation to confine the defence of slavery to mere negro slavery is very strong, for it is obvious that they require masters under all circumstances, whilst the whites need them only under peculiar circumstances, and those circumstances such as we can hardly realize the existence of in America. May the day never arrive when our lands

shall be so closely monopolized, and our population become so dense, that the poor would find
slavery a happy refuge from the oppression of capi-
tal. In the South, there is another and stronger
reason for the feeling of indignation at the bare
suggestion of white slavery—that is pride of caste.
No man loves liberty and hates slavery so cordially
as the Southerner . . . . Accustomed from childhood to connect the idea of slavery with the negro,
and of liberty with the white man, it shocks his
sensibilities barely to mention white slavery. 'Tis
vain to talk to him of the usages of mankind, for his
prejudices and prepossessions were formed long
before he heard of history, and they are too strong
to be reasoned away."

If Southerners led in expounding the *theory* of racial inequality, Northerners were not delinquent in
following the *practice* of racial inequality. In 1838,
when the drive to increase popular participation in
government was reaching its climax, Pennsylvania,
the locale of many eloquent expressions in behalf of
human equality, withdrew the right of suffrage from
its thriving free black population. In Vermont, where
the number of blacks was negligible, the government
barred them from military service. In Indiana, a likely
place for runaway slaves to escape to from the land of
bondage below the Ohio River, the legislature
enacted a law forbidding their entry. Even the antislavery societies themselves earnestly debated the
wisdom and propriety of admitting Negroes into
membership, and many of them decided against such
a policy!

Small wonder that the mere act of emancipation did little to promote the idea of equality. By the time that the Civil War was over, the purveyors of racism had done their work so well that the notion that blacks were inferior to whites was all but universal. Those who subscribed to the idea of full and complete equality and unlimited equality of opportunity represented a small and ineffectual minority of the American people. When Benjamin Butler, fresh from successfully pushing the Civil Rights Bill through Congress spoke in Cincinnati in 1875, a member of the audience asked if equal rights extended to saloons and similar places. "Goodness no," Butler replied, "after all, we white people must have *some* places where we do not have to be confronted by Negroes."

It was not merely the saloons where blacks were not wanted. It was also the schools, hospitals, churches, and cemeteries that held fast to the doctrine based on the belief of racial inferiority, that blacks and whites should not enjoy the fellowship and common experiences that equality implied. Soon, there would not even be the pretext of the Civil Rights Act to keep alive the fiction of the equal protection of the laws. After the act was declared unconstitutional in 1883, the limitless throngs who devoutly subscribed to the doctrine of inequality could practice their beliefs with impunity. When the Court declared that the Fourteenth Amendment did not authorize Congress to enact legislation to guarantee the equal protection of the laws of which the amendment spoke, one black leader declared ruefully, "We have been baptized in ice water." Even more distressing than the Court's legal justifications for declaring the Civil Rights Act unconstitutional, was the fact that the vast majority of Americans, North and South, did not believe that blacks had a right to equal accommodations in public places and their firm conviction that blacks should, somehow, remain for all time pariahs in the land of their birth and the land whose development and prosperity had been the special burden of blacks to bear for two centuries and more.

The practice of racial segregation and discrimination reached a fine art and reflected both originality and ingenuity as Americans made certain that blacks be kept in an inferior position. The self-fulfilling assertions of racial inferiority were made explicit in the state appropriations that provided several times more for the education of white children than for the education of black children. In 1900 Adams County, Mississippi, paid each Negro child the compliment of suggesting that $2.00 was adequate for his education, while $22.25 was necessary to educate each white child!

By the early years of the twentieth century each Southern state had not only systematically disfranchised its black citizens but had heaped on them every conceivable form of indignity, from segregation to intimidation and from discrimination to lynching. In the North, to which blacks went in ever-increasing numbers to escape the wrath of an unrepentant and uncompromising South, they soon discovered the doctrine of racial inequality was not confined to the South. The ghetto slums to which they were consigned, the places of public accommodation from which they were barred, the employment opportunities that often vanished when they presented themselves told a grim and sordid story of the corrosive effects of pervasive American racism.

These phenomena were not confined to the nineteenth century. Had that been the case, we would examine them as mere curiosities of a bygone age. But, unhappily, they became a part of the bitter legacy with which Americans would have to cope in the twentieth century. The problem of voting would not become amenable to solution until the 1960s; and large pockets of resistance would persist down into the 1980s. The problem of equality of opportunity in education would only begin to yield to effective resolution in the last decades of the twentieth century; and demographic patterns that reflected the flight of whites from communities in which their children might be exposed to common classrooms and common educational experiences with blacks indicated that neither school desegregation nor equal educational opportunity for blacks and whites was complete. Discrimination in employment and housing would require the resources and ingenuity of hosts of deeply committed workers to break through the thick layers of racial bigotry that had prevented their solution in preceding years. Only in our own time have Americans witnessed significant moves toward the achievement of full equality of opportunity; and only the blindest optimists or the most naive observers would suggest that equality of opportunity is at last at hand.

Meanwhile, what had happened to the dream of equality of opportunity? It would not die, and it is of those who helped to keep it alive that I wish to speak.

From the time that it was articulated as a worthy goal by some obscure and nameless colonists far back in the seventeenth century, it could always find some advocates. Even when it was renounced by those who had once stated the principles of equality so eloquently, there were others who took up the cause and vigorously agitated for its realization. When those most able and most likely to fight for equality failed to stand the test, there were others, often the least able and the least likely who, nevertheless, stood up for the cause and kept the dream alive.

It was Paul Cuffe who was among the first to remind the patriots in the 1770s that their fight for political independence was fatally flawed because their practice was inconsistent with their theory. They had declared that taxation without representation was tyranny, and this became the rallying cry of the movement for independence. "But what about us," Paul Cuffe asked, as he spoke for himself and the other free Negroes of Massachusetts who were taxed by the colony but were not permitted to vote or hold office. His question was ignored as irrelevant and unimportant. Consequently, he and his brother refused to pay their taxes and were promptly slapped in jail. How embarrassing it must have been to Sam Adams, John Adams, James Otis, and other revolutionary firebrands of Massachusetts who were calling on their compatriots to sacrifice everything for freedom from tyranny. Apparently it had not occurred to them that they had subscribed to a universal principle which, by its very nature, applied to blacks as well as whites. If the British were guilty of tyranny by taxing the colonies without giving them representation in

Parliament, so were the colonists guilty of taxing people who had no representation in the colonial legislature because they could not vote. And as Cuffe and his brother cooled their heels in a Massachusetts jail, the position of the Massachusetts revolutionaries was exposed in all its hypocritical inconsistency and absurdity. Shortly thereafter Massachusetts passed a law allowing its handful of free Negroes liable to taxation to vote and to enjoy the privileges belonging to other citizens. Under the circumstances, the patriots, in passing the law, acted begrudgingly and ungraciously. Exigency rather than commitment to principle had moved them to action. It was the outrage of young, affluent black Paul Cuffe that had shaken the revolutionary movement to its foundation and had forced an action that made the movement a bit more honest.

But the movement was not yet really honest. Not only had disfranchised free blacks been taxed with impunity, but many fighters for political freedom either held slaves or condoned the institution of slavery. If they did not see the inconsistency in their position, it was soon brought to their attention by their own slaves who, although deprived of their liberty, had not been deprived of their capacity to think logically. In 1774, obviously thinking of all the strong positions that the Massachusetts legislature had taken against England, a group of slaves wrote to the legislative representative from their community. In part they said:

"Your Petitioners apprehend we have in common with all other men a naturel right to our freedoms without Being depriv'd of them by our fellow men as we are a freeborn Pepel and have never forfeited this Blessing by aney compact or agreement whatever.

"But we were unjustly dragged by the cruel hand of power from our dearest friends and sum of us stolen from the bosoms of our tender Parents and from a Populous Pleasant and Plentiful country and Broght hither to be made slaves for Life in a Christian land . . . . We therefore Bage your Excellency and Honours will give this its deer weight and consideration and that you will accardingly cause an act of the legislature to be pessed that we may obtain our Natural right our freedoms."

Such petitions were disquieting to say the least, for they told the patriots things they did not wish to hear, things that challenged their commitment to equality and raised doubts about the credibility of their arguments against England.

Perhaps the revolutionary movement would have followed its own logic and abolished slavery except that the economic interest in slavery on the part of some colonists was much too great for them to permit such a step. Consequently, there followed the incredible spectacle of patriots fighting for their own freedom and denying it to others. The logic of their position, if there was any, led to their excluding blacks from the revolutionary army. Between mid-1775 and mid-1776 the several states and the military high command under George Washington officially closed the door to Negro enlistments. And it was not until it became difficult for the patriots to raise sufficient volunteer forces among whites, while the slaves were meanwhile beginning to accept the cordial invitation of the British to join them, that the United States saw fit to open up its own military forces to black fighters. Once more the concession to the principle of equality, if there was any, lacked both magnanimity and grace.

Because, then, at its birth, the United States was not true to its own philosophy of freedom and equality for all men, it would be erratic on the subject throughout the entire course of its history. That is why the principle of equality was not written into the Constitution. That is why so many Americans, North and South, were unwilling to speak out against slavery in the first third of the nineteenth century. That is why the nation was torn apart when considerable numbers of black and white Americans vowed, in the words of Lord Mansfield, that slavery was too odious to exist in a country that professed to be committed to equality.

The eloquent declarations by those who spoke for freedom and equality were in the best traditions of the quest for the American dream. The words of James Forten, Jr., spoken before the Ladies Antislavery Society of Philadelphia in 1836, are much to the point:

> "I love America; it is my native land. . . . I feel as one should who sees destruction, like a corroding cancer, eating into the very heart of his country, and would make one struggle to save her. . . . I long to see the day when not a slave shall be found resting under its shadow; when it shall play with the winds pure and unstained by the blood of 'captive millions.' [In seeking to destroy slavery] you

are not seeking the destruction of the Union; but to render it still stronger; to link it together in one universal chain of Justice, and Love, and Freedom."

James Forten was the mildest of men both in temperament and in speech. Not so the Reverend Henry Highland Garnet, the distinguished free black political and religious leader, who came closer to reasserting the delinquent spirit and tradition of the Founding Fathers. Speaking before the Buffalo Convention of Colored Citizens in 1843, he said:

"Brethren, arise, arise! Strike for your lives and liberties. Now is the day and the hour. Let every slave throughout the land do this and the days of slavery are numbered. Rather die freemen than live to be slaves . . . . Awake, awake, no oppressed people have secured their liberty without resistance."

Patrick Henry, with all of his extravagant utterances, never spoke more eloquently in behalf of freedom and equality!

When the nation was finally torn asunder in the spring of 1861, the black volunteers of Boston, New York, and Philadelphia could hardly believe their ears. No Negroes were to be taken into the Army of the United States! The men at the recruiting stations, taking orders from officials in Washington, sounded like they might be taking orders from officials in the Confederacy. This was *their* fight, the black volunteers had hoped. This was *their* opportunity to strike a blow and set their enslaved brethren free. Why, then, were they denied the opportunity? Because, simply stated, the slave states that had not seceded might be offended. More importantly, perhaps, it was because the white soldiers in the Union army did not wish to enjoy the pleasure of the company of black comrades in arms. Even more importantly, millions of Americans were not yet prepared to concede that the involvement of black soldiers and the emancipation of the slaves were inherent parts of the struggle to save the Union. It was the would-be black soldiers who, by offering their services and stating their feelings, indicated what the Civil War was all about. They declared that they were "ready to stand by and defend the government as the equals of white defenders—to do so with 'our lives, our fortunes, and our sacred honor' for the sake of freedom and as good citizens."

It was not until President Lincoln had issued the Emancipation Proclamation, and it was not until he thought that the use of black troops was a safe bet that blacks were permitted to take up arms in behalf of union and freedom. At last, after two years of pleading, blacks finally had the opportunity to fight slavery, oppression, and racism; and before it was over some 186,000 of them had enlisted in an outfit that was awkwardly called "United States Colored Troops." To fight for freedom and equality in a segregated army was bad enough; but to suffer discrimination in treatment and even in compensation was intolerable. White privates received $3.50 per month for clothing allowance, while black privates received $3.00. In view of this disparity in allowance, it was not clear what part of the uniform black soldiers were supposed to forgo. White privates received $13.00 per month as compensation while black privates received $7.00 per month. Negro soldiers were outraged. The 54th Massachusetts Regiment served a year without pay rather than accept discriminatory pay. One black sergeant in a South Carolina regiment was court-martialed and shot for "leading the company to stack arms before their captain's tent on the avowed ground that they were released from duty by the refusal of the government to fulfill its share of the contract." Finally, early in 1864 the War Department began to pay blacks the same as whites. Thus, slowly and painfully was the government of the United States brought to a semblance of honesty, decency, and equality even as it fought for its own survival. It was brought to this position by the relentless, persistent efforts of those who would not permit the principle of equality to die.

By the end of the Civil War, the American concept of equality was somewhat intact, despite the denial of equality by the people and in places where one might have expected more. It had been kept intact not by leaders like Thomas Jefferson or George Washington or Andrew Jackson or even by Abraham Lincoln. Instead, it remained a viable concept, thanks to people like Paul Cuffe, the humble black petitioners of Boston, Henry Highland Garnet, the black Union soldiers, the black abolitionists, and their white compatriots like William Lloyd Garrison and Wendell Phillips. But their spiritual legatees would have to do all that they possibly could to hold the concept of equality before the American people as a challenge to greatness in the century following emancipation.

After the Civil War the forces committed to the categorical denial of equality were powerful in the extreme. Since, to most Americans in the nineteenth century, there was no necessary connection between freedom and equality, many argued that the nation had discharged its obligation to freedom by emancipating the slaves. Furthermore, there were some new ideas taking hold in the land. Central among them was the notion that the government should have *no role* in securing or guaranteeing equality of all citizens. Rather, each individual was to work out his own destiny; and if one had the ability and resourcefulness, he made his own opportunities and worked his way to the top or wherever he wanted to go. If he did not have such qualities, he was doomed to some lower station in life more in keeping with his abilities. In a society where some persons, by virtue of race, were already at an almost hopeless disadvantage, these new doctrines did nothing more than justify their already lowly and degraded status.

The freedmen had their own concept of equality and of the obligation of the government to guarantee it. When one former Confederate state after another wrote constitutions that gave the vote to whites and withheld it from blacks in 1865 and 1866, the freedmen sprang into action. They told the President that it was strange indeed that the government of the United States would permit those to vote who had so recently borne arms *against* the Union while permit-

ting those to be barred from voting who had so recently fought to *save* the Union. Those who had sufficient
loyalty and courage to come to the aid of the Union in
time of war, they pleaded, should surely have the
privilege of exercising the franchise in time of peace.

When disfranchisement of the freedmen came—
after a few years of voting—and when segregation,
discrimination, and violence darkened their lives and
dashed their hopes, they kept the concept of equality
alive when so few others believed in it or worked for
it. When the Civil Rights Act of 1875 was declared unconstitutional by the Supreme Court in 1883 and
when the *New York Times* led in praising the decision,
it was Frederick Douglass who cried out once again
for decency and equality. He said:

> "Until this nation shall make its practice accord
> with its Constitution and its righteous laws, it will
> not do to reproach the colored people of this coun-
> try with keeping up the color line—for that people
> would prove themselves scarcely worthy of even
> theoretical freedom, to say nothing of practical
> freedom, if they settled down in silent, servile,
> and cowardly submission to their wrongs, from
> fear of making their color visible."

As the violence increased, with lynchings reaching
more than one hundred per year and race riots ceas-
ing to be uncommon, black Americans did begin to
despair. But as Douglass had counseled, their desperation did not silence them, nor did it constrain them
from speaking out for justice and equality. In 1905 a

group led by W.E.B. DuBois and calling themselves the Niagara Movement was uncompromising in the demands it made:

> "We believe that Negro American citizens should protest emphatically and continually against the curtailment of their rights. We believe in manhood suffrage; we believe that no man is so good, intelligent or wealthy as to be entrusted wholly with the welfare of his neighbor . . . . We refuse to allow the impression to remain that the Negro American assents to inferiority, is submissive under oppression and apologetic before insults."

That was the beginning—merely the beginning—of a movement organized and promoted by whites and blacks alike to challenge Americans to extend equality to all citizens. Soon, the National Association for the Advancement of Colored People would attract a great number of blacks and whites who believed that the process of degradation of Negroes was nothing less than the subversion of the American concept of equality. A bit later, still another group of whites and blacks organized the National Urban League to solve some pressing problems in the area of jobs and housing.

Within the span of a decade or so, dozens of lesser groups launched numerous programs looking toward improving the social order and more especially to achieve equality in the land. Some would be more radical, some more action-oriented, and some more conservative and more committed to persuasion. The large numbers of such groups and the wide variety of

approaches testify to the complexity of the problem
and its utter defiance of solution. Following World
War I there were scores of race riots, hundreds of
lynchings, countless practices of segregation and discrimination, and no end to studied insults and indig-
nities, all giving evidence of the strength of the re-
solve to deny equality to all Americans.

Those who continued to promote the concept of
equality during the last half century have had to cut
through the tough fiber of American racism by
challenges in the courts, struggles for protective legislation, boycotts, demonstrations, and appeals to justice and decency. That is what the Legal Defense and
Educational Fund of the NAACP, the National Urban
League, the Southern Christian Leadership Conference, People United to Serve Humanity, Martin
Luther King, Roy Wilkins, A. Philip Randolph,
Whitney Young, Jesse Jackson, and a host of others
have been doing as they have challenged our
democratic system to extend equality to all Americans.

During the past half century the quest for equality
has continued. There were times when it was so
ephemeral and remote as to make it nothing more
than a dream. There were times when it was so elu-
sive as to discourage any hope or prospect of realization. But, as in the earlier years of the history of this
country, those who carried on the quest were
successful in maintaining at least that the dream
would some day come true.

But no one is interested in pursuing a dream in-
definitely. It would be safe to say that two or three

centuries is just about long enough to pursue a goal, however worthy or engaging, unless there are some indications that the goal is clearly closer to realization. By this time in its history, moreover, this nation has all the resources and power to achieve almost anything in the field of human and race relations that it cares to achieve. And, after all, we do appear to be close enough to understanding the implications of equality to appreciate the parameters as well as its significance for our total social well-being. Where we *have* come close to equality, for example in important areas of human endeavors ranging from professional sports to segments of political life to certain advances in the world of business and industry, the consequences have not been disastrous, as some had feared. A black man became the head of the largest state system of higher education in the United States—the State University of New York—and there is no report that the system has declined. Blacks became mayors of Atlanta, Philadelphia, Los Angeles, New Orleans, and even Chicago without causing an earthquake in the political world. Black and white hard hats have worked together on construction jobs, and the buildings on which they worked did not collapse. Blacks have piloted commercial airlines without raising the level of danger in flying. There are numerous black superintendents of public schools, and their administrations have not adversely affected the development of those school systems.

In the areas where we have approached the goal of equality, the results have been encouraging to the believers and reassuring to the doubters. It has become quite clear that the role of dedicated fighters for

equality has been indispensable. Without the conviction that equality is a worthy pursuit and without the
will to pursue it, in season and out, there would never
have been even an approach to its realization. It has
also become clear that the commitment of important
institutions such as churches, schools, civic organizations, and the like has been extremely important.
Without their sustained and vigorous efforts, the
cause would have foundered on the shoals of a bicker-
ing, cantankerous, and aimless social order. Finally,
the role of government at all levels has been crucial
and continues to be so. The drive to involve government in adherence to the principles on which it is
built has been a new and important ingredient in the
struggle.

In more recent years, however, the federal government has declined to take a positive role in advancing
equality. The present administration was slow to express any interest whatever in the continuation of the
Voting Rights Act when it came up for renewal in
1982. It has been less than energetic in the
enforcement of that act, and in some instances has refused without explanation to pursue cases charging
the violation of the act that had been filed by the
previous administration. It has consistently opposed
the work of the Law Enforcement Assistance Administration that had been established to provide the
poor with representation in the courts in matters of
litigation. It has changed the purpose and function of
the United States Commission on Civil Rights from a
strong voice speaking out for the protection of civil
rights of minorities to an advocate for administration
policies that, at times, contradict the historic

purposes for which the Commission was established almost thirty years ago. It has opposed legal remedies or even informally using the prestige of the government to support measures to increase equal employment opportunities for blacks. It has taken an active interest in reversing hiring practices in both the public and private sectors where such practices looked toward increasing the number of blacks and other minorities through stated numerical goals or quotas. It has opposed the busing of school children as a means of desegregating the schools, and the President has gone so far as to visit communities and denounce busing even where it has been successful and where the community has enthusiastically supported the practice. It has advocated a reduction in support for school lunch programs, a reduction in aid to dependent children, and a curtailment of numerous other programs that aided minorities and the poor.

Democracy's slow, tortuous movement toward equality will have difficulty in sustaining the setbacks it has suffered in recent years. It took more than two centuries to get this country to accept the principle of equality for all men and move to the point where it would write the principle into such legislation as the Civil Rights Act of 1964 and the Voting Rights Act of 1965. It took the weight of the executive branch of the federal government to persuade, cajole, and lead the Congress and the nation to acquiesce in the view that inequality based on race has no place in America in the closing years of the twentieth century.

It cannot be argued, as the Attorney General of the United States has recently made a feeble attempt to do, that we must seek guidance for the government's role in social policy in the views set forth by the "founding generation." The founding generation did not have nuclear weapons or outer space or busing or ghettoes or slums or the Ku Klux Klan with which to contend. Those who wrote the Constitution failed to agree on a number of important issues and, at times, left the language of the Constitution vague in order to accommodate perplexing problems of the future. To shrink from the pressing task of deciding how best to solve some of the great issues of our time on the ground that the founding generation did nothing about them is, as Mr. Justice William J. Brennan, Jr., recently observed, "Little more than arrogance cloaked as humility." It is arrogant, he continued, "to pretend that from our vantage we can gauge accurately the intent of the Framers on application of principle to specific, contemporary questions . . . . A position that upholds constitutional claims only if they were within the specific contemplation of the Framers in effect establishes a presumption of resolving textual ambiguities against the claim of constitutional right. This is a choice no less political than any other; it expresses antipathy to claims of the minority to rights against the majority." Nothing better points up the dismaying direction in which equal rights have been pushed in recent times than the fact that a justice of the United States Supreme Court felt called upon to speak out against "arrogance cloaked as humility."

Even as we approach the bicentennial of the Constitution, we continue to be challenged to draw from the Constitution and the Bill of Rights those principles that will place equality within the reach of

all Americans. I speak here not of equality of condition but equality of opportunity, the chance to secure
a decent job, a decent house, adequate education, decent health care, and an environment that will not
choke us to death. This requires the active intervention of government, not especially for those who have
been fortunate in building up assets—often with the
assistance of government—but precisely for those
who have been the losers and, in many cases, have
been exploited by the more affluent.

The challenge to our democratic institutions, then,
is first to recognize the inequities that abound all
about us, and to realize that government has had
much to do with creating or facilitating these inequities through actions ranging from land grants to tax
rebates. The next step is to adopt policies and
programs that will reduce, even eradicate, the inequities resulting from advantages created or facilitated by
government intervention; and this can only be done
by government itself. The final step is to eliminate,
under government leadership, those practices and
policies that feed on inequality and, indeed, increase
the differences that already exist.

One can hope, one must hope, that in our own time
we can get sufficient hold of ourselves to shape our
own destiny as we will. If we can reorder our priorities so that we can create a society of equals, where
freedom abounds, where the riches we enjoy are
shared with the many thousands who are starving in
our midst, where we no longer take pride in having a
better school in one section of town than in another,
where equality stalks the land replacing bigotry, arrogance, and exploitation, we can show the world

something more powerful than even nuclear force. We can show it that peace and prosperity among peoples can indeed be achieved by peaceful means, and we can challenge them to go and do likewise.

AFFIRMATIVE ACTION *VERSUS* THE CONSTITUTION

by

Harvey C. Mansfield, Jr.

Harvey C. Mansfield, Jr.

Harvey C. Mansfield, Jr., is Professor of Government at Harvard University. He earned his A.B. in 1953 and his Ph.D. in 1961, both from Harvard, and taught at the University of California at Berkeley for two years before joining the Harvard faculty in 1962. He served as Chairman of the Department of Government from 1973 to 1977.

Professor Mansfield was awarded a Guggenheim Fellowship in 1970-71 and an NEH Fellowship in 1974-75. He was a member of the Council of the American Political Science Association in 1980-82 and a fellow of the National Humanities Center in 1982.

In addition to many articles in journals and books, Professor Mansfield is the author of Statesmanship and Party Government, A Study of Burke and Bolingbroke *(University of Chicago Press, 1965),* The Spirit of Liberalism *(Harvard University Press, 1978), and* Machiavelli's New Modes and Orders: A Study of the Discourses on Livy *(Cornell University Press, 1979). His edition of* Selected Letters of Edmund Burke *was published by University of Chicago Press in 1984.*

AFFIRMATIVE ACTION *VERSUS* THE CONSTITUTION

by

Harvey C. Mansfield, Jr.

Affirmative action is perhaps the most interesting policy issue of our day because it best reveals how we now understand our Constitution. How we understand our Constitution best reveals how we understand ourselves as a free people, what our condition is, and where we are tending. As an issue of public policy and as a question of constitutional law, affirmative action is important—but other such matters are also important, and some are more important. It is for what it reveals—a practical question containing and even asserting a theoretical understanding—that affirmative action has captured my interest. (See also my article, "The Underhandedness of Affirmative Action," *National Review*, May 4, 1984, pp. 27-32.) Even the phrase "affirmative action" is interesting. It seems redundant, for who would want a negative or passive action? But it implies that the business of government is to make things happen and not just to lie back and let them happen; indeed it implies a deliberate change of policy by government, in the way it secures our rights, from "negative action" to affirmative action. How does this change affect our Constitution?

Affirmative action has been in the news as at this writing (late 1985) the Reagan administration tries to make up its mind what to do about it. The Justice Department, under Attorney General Meese, is eager to rescind any requirement for affirmative action quotas by the federal government and in general to roll back and contain affirmative action to measures of encouraging recruitment of its beneficiaries short of goals and quotas. The Commerce and Labor departments, with no such overall concern, do not want to rock the boat and anger those whose support may be needed or neutrality desired in issues they consider more substantial. They represent those—including many Democrats as well as Republicans—who do not feel comfortable with affirmative action but do not want to fight it.

The last dramatic development in affirmative action was the Supreme Court's decision in June 1984, in *Firefighters v. Stotts,* that a federal court cannot require Memphis to ignore workers' seniority in making layoffs for the sake of affirmative action quotas. (104 S.Ct. 2576 [1984]. See "Toward an Understanding of *Stotts,*" U.S. Commission on Civil Rights, Clearinghouse Publication 85, January 1985.) Justice White's majority opinion contained a statement that relief could be provided under the Civil Rights Act "only to those who have been actual victims of illegal discrimination." (*Id.* at 2589.) Affirmative action, of course, provides relief to *presumed* victims of illegal discrimination without their having to show actual discrimination. If this statement should be applied to affirmative action in general—which is doubtful and disputed—it would call for a welcome return to the principle and language of the Civil Rights Act of 1964. As is well known, the act's legislative history contains a remark by one of its sponsors, Senator Hubert Humphrey, partially quoted by Justice White, denying that its intent was to set up a system of racial quotas or to achieve a racial balance.

One should note, however, that in this decision as in most discussion of affirmative action, the central question is one of *justice*, and the beneficiaries of affirmative action are referred to as *victims*. More and more, our legal system is coming to regard American citizens as victims rather than free agents and to substitute the imposition of punitive justice for the democratic choice of policy. The expansion and the transformation of tort law make this tendency apparent to all, as Americans increasingly sue and are sued not for wrongful acts—implying responsible actors—but for victimization in which the victims are treated as passive and uncomprehending recipients of injustice who are not expected to do or understand anything on their own. By a recent "consent decree," for example, Prudential Insurance Company was required to send an offer of free remedial training to 8,000 minority job applicants who had been rejected because they could not pass a test. This event sent, or should have sent, a shiver of fear into the hearts of teachers everywhere. Teachers, like other consumers, are used to demanding warranties from businessmen and corporations: when it doesn't work, pay me back! But when this idea is carried into teaching, the result is not so agreeable. Students or former students might insist on a warranty providing them relief for the consequences of any remaining stupidity or ignorance after they or their parents or the public have paid their tuition, and teachers might have to provide free remedial training or worse. In this situation, as with affirmative action in general, the law makes victims of the alleged victimizers. (For the victims of affirmative action, see Walter Berns, "Affirmative Action vs. the Declaration of Independence," *New Perspectives*, U.S. Commission on Civil Rights, Summer 1984, p. 27.)

Still, the most revealing incident regarding affirmative action remains the one by which the first Interior Secretary in the Reagan administration, James Watt, lost his job. He set off a furor by remarking that he had appointed to a coal-leasing board "a black, a woman, two Jews, and a cripple." It was a remark of shameless cynicism, but it was also true. He should have appointed the same people and not said why. He should have known, indeed he surely knew, that to state the true purpose of his appointments was to render them useless for that purpose. An affirmative-action appointment does not serve its purpose unless one denies that it has been made for that purpose. The denial is necessary in order not to hurt the pride of the beneficiary, because an affirmative-action appointment necessarily implies something lacking in the appointee. This lack, to be sure, is not the fault of the appointee—rather it is the fault of white, male America. But there is nonetheless a lack, and this must be denied. By failing to deny it, by telling the truth, Watt lost his job and thereby revealed for all to see that affirmative action is more a matter of pride than justice.

Proponents of affirmative action point to past injustices done to blacks and to other victims of American society who deserve this compensation partly for revenge and partly to enable them to take advantage of the new opportunities now available in American society. Opponents reply that one cannot remedy past injustice with new injustice; that with such group justice, one may benefit an individual who has not suffered at the expense of an individual who has not been guilty; and that affirmative action is thus in truth punitive justice rather than the distributive justice it claims to be. Still, regardless of the winner of this debate—even if affirmative action is just and is required by justice—this cannot be the only consideration. It remains a question whether it is good for blacks and other beneficiaries of affirmative action to regard themselves and to be regarded as victims. For as we see from the Watt incident, it seems a strange and unsatisfactory act of justice that cannot take pride in announcing whom it has benefited and why.

To see how affirmative action affects the Constitution, let us then consider it from the standpoint of pride. In what follows I shall confine myself to blacks, and leave aside women and Hispanics. Blacks are the only group that was brought to America against their will, then enslaved while here, and after being emancipated, held down in segregation as second-class citizens. Their case is quite different from that of women, who, I must say, suffered no such oppression. As proof of this hardy assertion I offer the great surrender of American males to the women's movement in the last two decades: no confrontation

such as at Little Rock or Selma; no Governor Wallace
to be a hero of the male chauvinist pigs. The women's
revolution has been accomplished by "raising consciousness"—first the consciousness of women, then
of men. But an oppression that can be overthrown by
complaints is hardly oppression. Though the Equal
Rights Amendment did not pass, this was more because women did not agree about it than because men
opposed it; and if now the women's movement is
changing its character in a "second stage," from
unisex to job and motherhood, this too is because
women are having second thoughts about their own
first thoughts. As for Hispanics, they have come to
America voluntarily and are making great strides except to the extent that they are hindered by programs
of bilingualism. Their difficulties, and those of other
minorities as well as the female majority, do not belong in the same category as the wrongs done to
blacks.

The advantages of affirmative action might appear
to be the following. First, it is revenge for the denial
of the birthright of blacks as Americans. That
birthright of full citizenship with civil and political
rights was first expressly then tacitly taken away, and
whites now should have to pay for this. Revenge is not
very pretty, but it is very human; and most criminals
are punished for lesser crimes than enslaving other
human beings. Revenge, usually under the name of
"compensation" or "reparation," is certainly part of
the appeal of affirmative action to blacks.
    Second, one must face the fact of black insistence
on affirmative action. This program, which was not in-

vented by them but invented for them by whites, is now *their* program, their right, their entitlement. To abandon it now would be a "takeaway," a reaction against the progress achieved by the Civil Rights Movement, perhaps even a sign that this progress was never really secure, that whites were never really serious about civil rights. As one who has spoken on affirmative action at universities, I can testify that this feeling is very strong among the most educated blacks, including black students. The black community, as defined by those who speak for it—which is the effectual definition of a community—is in favor of affirmative action. Any politician who speaks against affirmative action is understood as not interested in appealing, or at least as not appealing, to blacks. Thomas Kean, the recently reelected Republican governor of New Jersey, spoke in favor of affirmative action during his campaign and came away with 60 percent of the black votes. What he said was understood by black voters as an appeal to them, was so intended by Governor Kean, and was well received by them.

Third, affirmative action enables blacks to learn and improve by doing. They can bypass the slow system of apprenticeship in which many get bogged down while gaining allegedly necessary qualifications. They can learn on the job and take pride in acting on their own and doing by themselves instead of always submitting to tests that have been laid down by others. These tests, together with the whole system of "qualifications," it is often said, were not imposed on whites when they were on top or making their way to the top. The whites on top had the old-boy network, and the immigrant whites on the rise had informal control

of certain jobs, such as the Irish in the police force.
Affirmative action for blacks merely makes public and
formal policy of preferential practices that were not
found so objectionable, or are not objected to today,
when done by whites. Besides, so-called "unqualified" appointments are often good ones, and "qualified" characters often turn out incompetent.

Fourth, blacks can become responsible Americans
by getting their share of the best jobs and highest
positions in America. They will be proud to be Americans when they are respected, for *respect* is the essential thing, not money or standard of living. When
blacks are respected, America can then respect her-
self and no longer suffer guilt for the American dilemma. The gap between America's ideals and the American reality is essentially revealed in her treatment of
blacks.

Those are the advantages of affirmative action;
nonetheless, there are disadvantages, which, I believe, outweigh them. To begin, we should return to
the necessity that affirmative-action programs must
conceal the help they render to their beneficiaries.
Such programs cannot claim success, we have seen,
because to do so would insult those whom they have
just benefited. One does not see a smiling executive
introduce "our new affirmative-action appointment"
to his fellow employees. Affirmative action beneficiaries are in self-contradiction: They deserve the
help of affirmative action because they are equal; but
they need it because they are not equal. The only way
out is to accuse the rest of American society of racism
in order to explain why potential equality does not be-

come actual. Surely it is true that racial prejudice remains in America, but it is almost as sure that it will not be cured by accusation. To whom does one make an accusation of racism? To people who believe racism to be a bad thing, not to racists. Thus the very accusation that America is racist presupposes that most Americans are not racist. In consequence, accusations of racism are not really believed by those who accuse, and they tend to become routine. An example is the accusation of "institutional racism," where actual racists are not sought, let alone named. Well, this is no way to get on with one's fellow citizens. These accusations deny the real progress that has been made, and they overlook the real goodwill most Americans have for blacks, the admiration for their courage and endurance, and the genuine longing for community with this wronged people. Affirmative action does not find racism but imputes it to Americans as the sole cause of remaining inequalities. It claims to be a temporary program, but it sets no limit on itself other than the eradication of prejudice, that is, the achievement of perfection in human community. Meanwhile, the benefits of affirmative action depend on imperfection—on the continuance of racism as asserted in accusations of racism. We might suspect that those accusations will continue as long as the benefits of affirmative action are desired. But with a view to the bureaucracy that has been created to enforce affirmative action, both in government and with employers, we can be *sure* that they will continue out of both self-interest and professional duty. Affirmative action lives and thrives in an atmosphere of poison. It wants to make us less conscious of race by the route of making us more conscious of it. On the face of it, to reach that goal by this route is not likely.

Second, affirmative action tends to make blacks irresponsible by encouraging them to blame others for their difficulties. It is of course not always incorrect to blame others for your troubles, but it is almost always counterproductive to do so. You cannot easily reform those whom you blame, but you can do something about yourself. Blacks can and should take responsibility for what they can do, even against the hostility of the white majority (to the extent that this majority is truly hostile). What blacks can do is limited, but this is the case with all human actions, and responsible action includes accepting what one cannot do so as to do what one can. Blacks, therefore, should not wait around for whites to take affirmative action to change their attitudes when blacks can change their own attitudes by affirming their own actions. The problems of blacks are not going to be solved by whites; indeed, it is better that they not be. This truth has been recognized recently by several thoughtful blacks—Jeff Howard, Ray Hammond, and particularly, Glenn C. Loury. (Jeff Howard and Ray Hammond, "Rumors of Inferiority," *The New Republic*, September 9, 1985, pp. 17-21. Glenn C. Loury, "A New American Dilemma," *The New Republic*, December 31, 1984, pp. 14-18; "Beyond Civil Rights," *The New Republic*, October 7, 1985, pp. 22-25; "The Need for Moral Leadership in the Black Community," *New Perspectives*, Summer 1984, pp. 14-19.) And, of course, Booker T. Washington long ago made it the centerpiece of his doctrine.

Affirmative action also leads to a patronizing, condescending attitude in whites toward blacks. Blacks are not held by whites to the same standards as other whites because they are not expected to perform as well. For if one expected as much from blacks as from whites, there would be no need for affirmative action. So affirmative action tends to confirm the idea of black inferiority in the minds of whites even while its purpose is to erase it. Blacks tend to get preferences of the kind that do them no good because they serve as excuses. Blacks, for example, are hired as affirmative-action officers rather than in jobs that lead somewhere. Charles Murray has rightly called this frame of mind "the new racism," and it is found in people who could never bring themselves to utter a racial slur. Blacks are said to be equal, but as a practical matter are held to be inferior. (Murray, "Affirmative Racism," *The New Republic*, December 31, 1984, pp. 18-23.) Derek Bok's answer to Murray's argument ("Admitting Success," *The New Republic*, February 4, 1985, pp. 14-16) asks whether equal opportunity, if returned to now, would produce any more progress for blacks than the little it accomplished before 1965 (i.e., before affirmative action). I think it would, because of the decline of racism, the success of the Civil Rights Movement, and the passage of the Civil Rights Act of 1964. But at some point, and why not now?, it is necessary to put confidence in blacks themselves.

As a result of blaming others and of being patronized by whites, blacks come to think of themselves as victims, hence as essentially passive. The solution seems to be, then, to make claims on white America

on the basis of their sufferings, needs, and wants—in
sum, on the basis of their inadequacies. But, instead
of regarding themselves as victims, blacks should
think of what they can *contribute* to America, and
make claims (for all of us make claims) on the basis of
what they have contributed and can now contribute.
Affirmative action makes blacks accentuate the negative and appear helpless in order to build a case for
aid, but in fact blacks have made many contributions
to American culture. They have played a dominant
role in our popular culture for some time, and their
intellectual leaders, such as Washington, Douglass,
and DuBois, are worthy of more appreciation and
study than they receive. Blacks should think of the
contributions they have made, and then think them
over: What does the black community want to contribute to America? This is thinking positively, and it
can be done only by blacks for themselves. But, as an
example of thinking it over, an outside observer might
ask whether it is such a good thing for educated blacks
to rush into the professions from which they have
been excluded, such as medicine and law, and also
into business—but forget the traditional professions
in the black community. It used to be that preacher
and teacher were the only professions open to blacks,
yet these two were very important to the dignity and
morale of the black community. Now they are not so
well respected as before, with consequences possibly
detrimental to blacks. For the sake of American education in general, I particularly worry about the minute number of blacks studying to become college
teachers.

The black community has indeed become wedded

to affirmative action, but is this a good thing? It is not necessarily permanent, as a recent poll in *Public Opinion* (Linda S. Lichter, Aug.-Sept. 1985) has shown that while 77 percent of black leaders favor affirmative action, the same percentage of their followers oppose it. I do not interpret this to mean that black leaders are not leaders of the black community, because leaders should lead, not follow; but it does suggest that if affirmative action is unwise, black leaders are not bound to it by the demands of their constituents. In their present determination black leaders clearly see affirmative action as a measure of their power; but it has to be said that the same thing is seen by most whites as a sign of their dependency. Reinforcing this appearance of dependency is the political isolation of blacks. In the 1984 presidential election two-thirds of the whites voted for President Reagan, but nine-tenths of the blacks voted for the Democratic candidate. Blacks have become conspicuous as the most loyal adherents of the Democratic party; they have become, as the Congressional Black Caucus says, the soul of that party. While there is nothing wrong in favoring one party rather than the other, there is disadvantage in doing so when a group can be so readily identified as privileged dependents or a "special interest." This is especially true when a different opinion is taken for disloyalty to the black community. Those few black leaders who oppose affirmative action have had to suffer for it in their standing with other blacks for having betrayed the common interest. (See the remarks of Bayard Rustin in *New Perspectives*, Winter 1985, p. 31.)

When that common interest is defined as affirmative action, the idealism of the Civil Rights Movement in its heyday is transformed into the defense of rights and privileges in jobs, positions, and offices. Its nobility is lost in calculation of mundane advantage. Since it is hard for blacks to work up enthusiasm for affirmative action in anyone else, they turn to making alliances with women and Hispanics. Let others in on affirmative action, and blacks will have a stronger political base, even a majority, to support them. But such alliances dilute the special case that blacks can reasonably make on their own behalf to the conscience of the nation. All too often, affirmative action produces jobs for white, middle-class women—a group that has never been enslaved or even underprivileged. It is true that there is nothing particularly shocking in politicking to protect one's self-interest, and the immigrant and other groups have in the past established informal, do-it-yourself affirmative-action programs. But it is also true that there is nothing edifying in such practices. Though some have attempted to justify them, no one has attempted before now to dignify them. On the contrary, every movement called "reform" has opposed and tried to uproot them. Those who have criticized the reformers, for example political scientists who find hidden merit in big city "corruption" in the good old days, have not proposed a formal program of "corruption" to help us return to those golden times. Instead, they have counseled prudence and a greater willingness to let things be and let things happen. In this spirit, one can see an obvious difference between the prudence of using black policemen in black neighborhoods, for example, and the erection of a formal requirement that this concession to human nature be generalized and insisted on as if it were a moral principle. If it is asked why blacks should not benefit as much as whites from such a concession, the answer is that they do: look at big-city government today.

The last disadvantage of affirmative action sums up all the others. Affirmative action makes blacks conspicuously dependent on the rest of America by becoming dependent on government. Blacks are not alone in this; all of us have become more dependent on so-called "entitlements." But blacks have become more so, for affirmative action is the most outstanding example of an entitlement.

What are entitlements, and what's the matter with them? In the narrow, technical sense, an entitlement is a budget item that cannot be reduced or contained by the process of budget control because the law awards it without reference to the number who claim it or qualify for it, thus without reference to the amount it will cost. But the term "entitlement" has escaped into American politics and even into political philosophy. There it designates a right whose exercise is guaranteed, to a certain degree, by the government. What does this mean?

The U.S. Constitution is based on rights that are prior to itself. These rights are secured by government and exercised by citizens in their private capacity; for example, the government secures the right of free speech by preventing interference with it, but it does not tell the citizen what to say or how to exercise his right. This distinction between the right and its exercise is the basis for the distinction between public and private or between state and society which constitutes a liberal democracy. By means of this distinction, government is limited because it acts for society, that is, for citizens in their private capacities; it facilitates the exercise of those capacities but does not prescribe how they are to be exercised. Government remains limited insofar as it maintains and respects the distinction between securing rights, which is the business of government, and exercising them, which is not.

The distinction between rights and their exercise is essential to limited government, but it can leave a situation in society in which limited government seems imperfect and incomplete. A limited government, for example, might make it illegal for any employer to discriminate on grounds of race in hiring, but it would not require employers to hire blacks since this would infringe upon their freedom to contract. So to a black, an equal right to a job might seem merely formal: The government does not secure him an actual job, only the right to compete for one where, without any overt act of discrimination, prejudice may effectually exclude him. Then, he might ask, why should not America live up to its ideals? And why should not government close the gap between its ideals and its reality? The Constitution is indeed based on rights, but rights are not rights unless one can exercise them effectually. The right and its exercise must be brought together so that the ideal becomes real and profession becomes fact. Thus, instead of "equal protection of the laws" as in the Fourteenth Amendment, one must provide "laws protecting equality." (For this distinction, see Jeremy Rabkin, "A

Civil Rights Snare," *New Perspectives*, Winter 1985, p. 4.) Affirmative action by government is necessary to close this gap because minorities and women have a background of disadvantage that keeps them from exercising their rights effectually.

"Background" is the key to this argument. One's background is commonly distinguished as both nature and nurture. "Nature" is the human capacities we have, plus the innate bent and talent of each individual. "Nurture" is the custom and history of one's group and nation, plus individual upbringing. The political philosophy behind limited government affirms that nature is more important than nurture; that humans have a fixed nature enabling them to overcome a background of poverty or deprivation. With the equipment of nature and given the chance to succeed, an individual can overcome, perhaps even disregard, the past history of his nation and long experience with oppression. Since his identity is more in this equipment, which is a positive capacity, than in his history, which may have been unfortunate, he has the means, as we say, for a "fresh start." In general, America has claimed to be, and has been to some extent, a fresh start for mankind, the New World. (While the American polity contains ethnic groups, it does not *define* itself in terms of ethnic origin. This is the beginning point of Nathan Glazer's classic study of affirmative action, *Affirmative Discrimination*, New York: Basic Books, 1975, p. 7.) In this view, the individual must be given the chance to succeed, as I said, by removing barriers to advancement characteristic of feudal or status societies which make more of one's conventional than one's natural advantages. Because of these natural advantages, liberal political philosophy holds, a disadvantaged individual does not need to be put on his feet by government, much less given a push in the right direction. He can pull himself up by his own bootstraps, which means, of course, with the aid of family and friends. The dominance of nature over nurture provides the basis for the liberal argument for equal opportunity and limited government. "Limited government" implies that government should not be used as much as it might be, and "equal opportunity" implies that not all succeed, or not all equally. Politically, then, the promise is for a series of partial reforms that open up opportunities but do not attempt to make everyone happy.

Affirmative action, however, comes from a political opinion and a philosophy that are not satisfied with partial reforms. It wants to close the gap between the ideal and reality, and to do so it understands a right not as a formal opportunity that may or may not succeed, but as an effectual guarantee from government, an entitlement. In the view of its supporters, partial reforms are no use because every extension of rights is canceled by the inability of those with a disadvantaged background to exercise their new rights, which to the supporters means, to exercise them equally. For them, only absolute reform is real reform. Real reform requires government action not merely against discriminatory actions but against the attitudes behind those actions.

When government proposes to change, or rather, *attack* attitudes, it encounters the right to consent, the basic right in the Constitution. Consent is the basic right because all other rights depend on it. Without the right of consent, other rights are merely the gift of the government, possibly to be withdrawn at the government's convenience. The right of consent is the right by which, when it is exercised to establish a constitution, other rights pass from *natural* rights (or human rights) to *civil* rights, rights enforceable by law that are more limited but more effectually protected than abstract natural rights. The right to consent is a matter of justice, because it is just to count each person as one. But it is also a matter of pride, for to count as one, each person must count *for* something, must be *worth* something. The right of consent presupposes that each adult is worthy of being taken seriously as a rational creature capable of choice, hence worthy of being persuaded and not taken for granted. His dignity requires that his consent be sought through persuasion, and neither ignored nor presumed. Affirmative action both ignores and presumes. Usually enforced by the judiciary, the branch that is furthest from consent, it ignores white males because they are presumed to be racist and it presumes on the consent of blacks and women because of their race and sex. Affirmative action is not yet fully applied to voting, but there is a trend in that direction. In the Voting Rights Act of 1982, Congress flirted with the idea of giving protected groups the representation it presumed they should vote for: black representatives for blacks, and so forth. This attempt at mandated racist voting was narrowly and only partially defeated. (See Abigail Thernstrom, " 'Voting Rights' Trap," *The New Republic*, September 2, 1985, pp. 21-23.)

Our problem is not the gap between the ideal and reality; this gap is *within* our ideal. It was deliberately

planned and fixed in our Constitution. It arises from
the right of consent, since that right both obliges us to
respect the rights of others and enables us to insist on
our own. That right, therefore, serves to perfect our
rights, but also permits prejudiced resistance to
progress. Government can attempt perfection by
overriding prejudice, but when it does so it can
develop a self-serving tyrannical—or bureaucratic!—definition of perfection. More important and
more urgent for us, it makes its citizens depend on
government for their rights, for the entitlements we
are beginning to take for granted. A free society is
necessarily imperfect; if it became perfect, citizens
would no longer have to exert themselves to be free.
What is affirmative action but an attempt by government in its least consensual branches, the bureaucracy and the judiciary, to redo what the Civil Rights
Movement did voluntarily and on its own respon-
siblity? Surely the contrast is remarkable between the
free, popular movement that led to the Civil Rights
Act of 1964 and the arbitrary, bureaucratic misinter-
pretation of that act which gave rise to affirmative action. Affirmative action may or may not be "unconstitutional" because it violates a clause of the Constitution, but in the broader sense it is unconstitutional
because it undermines the basic principles of our
Constitution.

MINORITY ADMISSION POLICIES AND PROCEDURES: ACCESS TO THE PROFESSIONS

by

Stanley M. Johanson

Stanley M. Johanson

Stanley M. Johanson holds the Bryant Smith Chair in Law at the University of Texas at Austin, where he teaches courses in Estate Planning and Wills & Estates. He was a Teaching Fellow at the Harvard Law School from 1961 to 1963, and has taught at the University of Texas since 1963. He was a visiting professor at the UCLA Law School 1967-68 and has been a summer visiting professor at a number of universities in the United States.

Professor Johanson earned his B.S. with High Honors in engineering at Yale University in 1955. In 1958 he received an LL.B. from the University of Washington, where he was Editor-in-Chief of the Washington Law Review and a member of the Order of the Coif, and in 1963 he received an LL.M. from Harvard Law School.

At the University of Texas at Austin, Professor Johanson is Chairman of the Law School Admissions Advisory Committee and of the AALS Annual Meeting Committee. He has won Teaching Excellence Awards in 1968, 1972, and 1973. He serves as Chairman of the Short Course on Estate Planning for The Southwestern Legal Foundation and is a frequent lecturer at Continuing Legal Education programs and taxation conferences. He is a member of the Law School Admission Council, an Advisor on the Restatement (Second) of Property of the American Law Institute, and an Academic Fellow of the American College of Probate Counsel. He is a member of the Texas, Washington (state), and American Bar Associations and serves as Chairman of the Board of Directors of the Tarrytown United Methodist Church Endowment Fund.

In addition to numerous articles on estate planning, will and trust drafting, and community property, Professor Johanson is the author of Family Wealth Transactions: Wills, Trusts & Estates *(with J. Dukeminier) and* Estate Planning: Problems and Materials.

MINORITY ADMISSION POLICIES AND PROCEDURES: ACCESS TO THE PROFESSIONS

by

Stanley M. Johanson

Although the title of my paper refers to "Access to the Professions" (stated in the plural), I shall confine my remarks to the legal profession, as it is the professional group with which I am most familiar. At the same time, I am hopeful that there may be some crossover value, and that my observations may also relate to the other professions, to their professional schools, and to their admission policies and procedures.

I would like to begin by relating a personal story. Thirty years ago, I applied for admission to the University of Washington School of Law, in Seattle. I was admitted.

While this favorable decision was personally very satisfying, gaining admission represented no great achievement on my part. Put simply, I was admitted to the law school because I had applied. Everyone (or nearly everyone) who applied for admission to that law school in 1955, and in all the preceding years, and in the years that immediately followed, was granted admission. To be sure, there may have been a few applicants who did not have the required 2.0 under-

graduate grade-point average on a 4.0 point scale (a C
average), but even that requirement could be waived
by the law school's dean. Perhaps there were also
some applicants who did not have the required college degree. However, many schools at that time did
not even require a college degree. A number of
schools granted admission at the end of the junior
year in college, with the first year of law school counting as the fourth year required for the baccalaureate
degree.

The admission experience at the law school I
attended was not an isolated phenomenon. (See
Abrahamson, *The LSAT for the 21st Century*, 34 J.
LEGAL EDUCATION 407 [1984].) This was the pattern
at all but a handful of the most prestigious law schools,
which, even then, received more applications from
qualified candidates than they could accommodate.
But remember: the unsuccessful applicants to those
more selective schools could, if they wanted to, gain
admission to some other law school. The upshot was
that any college graduate with a C average could find
a law school to which he or she would be admitted.
Most American law schools had an "open admission"
policy. Admission was open to all, or virtually all, college graduates. You had a *chance* to become a lawyer
. . . if you could manage to graduate from law school.
Not everyone did. A sizeable number of students
washed out, or were washed out, especially during
the first year.

I don't know how many older graduates from how
many schools have told me how, during one of their
first days in law school, their Torts professor, or per-

haps it was their Contracts professor, fixed a hard glare on the cowering multitude and said, "Look to your left and look to your right. Only one of you will still be here three years from now." Mercifully, that was an exaggeration, albeit only a slight exaggeration. At the law school that I attended, about one-half of those who began law school in the fall of 1955 were still around to graduate three years later. Such data as we have for that time indicate that, nationally, around 60 to 70 percent of all law-school entrants went on to graduate. In that era, law school admission procedures were not involved in the gatekeeping function of controlling access to the legal profession. Rather, the culling process took place in the law school itself (especially during the first year), and on the bar examination.

There was a certain populist appeal to such an open-admission policy. Virtually any college graduate had a chance to obtain a legal education and thus become a lawyer. You could attend law school. Whether you came out swimmingly or sank to the bottom— well, that was up to you.

At the same time, this open admission policy had its costs. There were the dollar costs of providing facilities and logistical support for more students than the school would graduate. For tuition-driven schools, there was something unseemly about collecting tuition from a large number of persons who would be booted out of school after one or two years. Finally, there were human costs, in terms of the large number of young men and the smaller number of women who were branded as failures because they couldn't cut it.

Remember, it was the successful students, not the less fortunate ones, who liked to tell that story about "looking to your right and looking to your left."

But that was thirty years ago. How times have changed! Law-school applications increased gradually but steadily until the late 1960s, when both the number of applicants and law-school enrollments literally exploded. Ever-increasing numbers of young (and not-so-young) men, and especially young (and not-so-young) women, began to apply to an increasing number of law schools. Consider these statistics. In the fall of 1955, I was one of 16,000 first-year law students in the nation's 122 ABA-accredited law schools; 9,600 of those students were graduated three years later. In 1963, there were 21,000 first-year law students, 13,000 of whom were graduated in 1966. In 1969, there were 29,000 first-year students; 22,000 were graduated three years later. In 1975, there were 39,000 first-year students, 33,000 of whom were graduated in 1978. Enrollment levels have stayed relatively constant since 1975. In the fall of 1984, there were 41,000 first-year students at the nation's 174 ABA-accredited law schools. (See American Bar Association Section on Legal Education and Admission to the Bar, REVIEW OF LEGAL EDUCATION IN THE UNITED STATES [1969, 1984].)

In 1955, I was one of 10,000 applicants who took the Law School Admission Test, which had been developed in 1947. (White, *LSAC/LSAS: A Brief History*, 34 J. LEGAL EDUCATION 369 [1984].) At its inception, the purpose of the LSAT was to enable the selective schools to identify candidates who were not qualified for law studies. It was not until later, when nearly all law schools became selective schools, that the LSAT was used to differentiate among candidates all of whom were qualified for law studies.

Thus while I was required to take the test as a condition to being admitted, my test score was not a factor in the admission decision. The school that I attended (as with many others at the time) was merely gathering data for possible use of the LSAT as an admission tool in future years. The fact that there were 16,000 first-year students in 1955 but only 10,000 LSAT test administrations demonstrates that many law schools did not require the test as part of the admission process.

In 1962, there were 26,000 test administrations; in 1969, 60,500. By 1975, all accredited law schools were using the LSAT as an integral part of the admissions process. In that year, there were 135,000 test administrations—more than twice as many as in 1969. This does not mean that there were 135,000 law school applicants in 1975. That figure reflects the total number of test administrations for the year, and includes persons who took the test two or more times. By 1975, admission to law school had become so competitive that it was not uncommon for an applicant to take the test several times in an effort to improve his or her admission credentials. Also, a number of persons who take the LSAT do not apply to any law school, even though their credentials might have gained them admission. While we do not know the exact number of applicants in 1975, our best judgment is that there were between 80,000 and 85,000 applicants—for 39,000 available seats. The days of open admission were over. Nearly all of the nation's law schools, and not just the more prestigious schools, were receiving applications from far more qualified applicants than they could accommodate. The era of selective admission practices was upon us.

These statistics from The University of Texas School of Law illustrate how rapidly admission credentials, and the quality of law-school student bodies, increased. The median credentials of the fall 1970 first-year class were a 2.92 undergraduate grade-point average and a 607 (73rd percentile) LSAT score. An enrollee with these credentials was predicted to graduate in the middle of his or her class. In 1970, any resident applicant with a 3.0 undergraduate grade-point average and an LSAT score of 505 (37th percentile) gained admission to The University of Texas. Correspondingly, an applicant with a 2.2 grade-point average needed a test score of 635 (81st percentile) to gain admission; and a candidate with a 3.5 grade-point average—regardless of the undergraduate institution attended—was admitted if he or she scored 430 (17th percentile) on the LSAT.

Five years later, the median grade-point average of the 1975 entering class at The University of Texas was 3.53, and the median LSAT score was 640 (80th percentile). Had a student with these credentials enrolled in the fall of 1970, he would have been in the top twenty percent of all enrollees. By 1975, an enrollee with these credentials was predicted to graduate in the middle of the class.

For the 1985 entering class at The University of Texas, the median undergraduate grade-point average was still 3.5, but the median LSAT score was 39 (87th percentile). (In 1982, the LSAT underwent substantial modification, including a change in the score scale from 200-800 to 10-48. A score of 39 is in the same percentile as a 670 score on the old scale.)

Consider, then, the plight of the applicant with a 3.0 grade-point average and a 505 LSAT score. Applying to The University of Texas in 1970, he was welcomed with open arms. Five years later, if academic credentials alone were considered in the admission decision, the candidate was not likely to gain admission at all.

On occasions when I have presented figures such as these at alumni gatherings, more than a few graduates—now successful lawyers—have told me, half-jokingly, that they probably wouldn't be admitted to law school if they were to apply today. My standard response has been a tactful one: "You must remember that there has been grade inflation at the college level since your day; your undergraduate grade point average probably would have been higher. Besides, if the admissions process had been as competitive then as it is now, you probably would have worked harder to compile a stronger gpa, and you would have taken the Law School Admission Test more seriously." A more candid response would be: "You are probably right."

Not surprisingly, the demise of open admissions was accompanied by a sharp decline in the number of academic failures. At most schools, the quality of the chosen applicants was such that they were virtually certain to demonstrate that they could handle whatever the law school dished out. With a student body comprised almost entirely of B+ and A students, more than a few of whom possessed Phi Beta Kappa keys and graduate degrees, successful performance in law

school—or at least passing work—was a foregone conclusion. Law schools continued to grade on the curve,
but this simply meant that the competition to reach
the upper end of the curve became more intense.
Many students whose prior academic work had placed
them in or near the top 10 percent of their class faced
the emotional adjustment of being pegged as "average" law students. Flunking grades, and the dismal
bluebooks that produced them, became less common.
At The University of Texas today, the attrition
rate—for all causes, not just academic failures—is less
than 3 percent.

What caused the stunning increases in law school
applications and enrollments over the last thirty
years? Various forces were at work. The products of
the postwar baby boom had reached college age. This,
coupled with rising affluence and rising aspirations,
resulted in a higher proportion of a larger population
attending and graduating from college. As college
enrollments stabilized after the baby-boomers passed
through the system, there was a reduction in the
number of new positions on college faculties. Liberal-
arts graduates who, in an earlier era, might have pursued a master's degree or a doctorate in their discipline, found law school a more promising graduate-
school alternative. Persons who had already obtained
M.A.'s or Ph.D.'s discovered that their degrees were
not marketable. A return to school—this time law
school—offered an acceptable way out of a bad situation. At another level, the idealism of the post-
Kennedy era, the emergence of the civil rights

movement, and agitation over the Viet Nam conflict made law school, and the opportunity to work change through the legal system, attractive to a number of young people. (See Zimmer, *Survival After the Boom: Managing Legal Education for Solvency and Productivity*, 34 J. LEGAL EDUCATION 437 [1984].)

The single most important factor, however, involved nothing less than a social revolution. Women discovered law school and the legal profession. In 1963, one out of twenty-six of the nation's law students was female. By 1969, the proportion had increased to one out of fifteen; in 1975, to one out of four; and in 1980, to one out of three. Today, 40 percent of the nation's law students are women. Even more remarkably, while enrollments have risen, the number of males attending law school has actually declined. In 1972, 90,000 out of 102,000 law students were males. In 1982, law school enrollments had increased to 128,000—but only 81,000 of those students were males.

Finally, a portion of the increase in enrollments is attributable to the subject of our concern today: There has been an increase in minority enrollments.

These dramatic increases in law school enrollments have led to a corresponding increase in the number of lawyers in the United States. Census data reflect that there were approximately 211,000 lawyers (including judges) in the United States in 1960. Barely 1 percent of them were blacks or Hispanics. By 1970, the number of lawyers had grown to 260,000, 5,000 of whom were members of the minority groups I have mentioned. In 1980, there were 530,000 lawyers in the United States—the number of lawyers had doubled in ten years. Of these, 15,300 (2.9 percent) were blacks and 9,500 (1.8 percent) were Hispanics.

These demographic data tell us three things. First, the law business has been and still is a growth industry. Over the past two decades, the growth in the number of lawyers, both in absolute terms and in proportion to the population, has been astonishing. In 1960, there was one lawyer for every 850 persons in the United States. In 1980, the ratio was one lawyer for every 425 persons. Today, there are over 650,000 lawyers in the United States, and it is estimated that there will be close to a million lawyers by the turn of the century.

Second, the proportion of black and Hispanic lawyers has grown both in absolute numbers and in proportion to the overall population: from 5,000 in 1970 to just under 25,000 in 1980. As is explained more fully below, this did not just happen.

There is, however, a third conclusion to be derived from these data. While there has been an increase in the number of black and Hispanic lawyers, they still represent a small proportion of the legal profession. According to 1980 census data, blacks and Hispanics comprise 18 percent of the nation's population, yet they represent fewer than 5 percent of the nation's lawyers.

What have the law schools done about this situation? What should they be doing about it?

I return briefly to my personal story. There were two blacks in my first-year law class at the University of Washington in 1955. Both of them were graduated,

as I was, three years later. It may be more than anec-
dotal to note that one of them is now a federal judge
on the United States Court of Appeals for the Ninth
Circuit. The other is a trial judge in the state of Washington.

How many minority students were there in all the
nation's law schools in 1955? We don't know, because
nobody was counting. We do know, however, that the
number was miniscule. At The University of Texas (as
was true of many schools in the South and Southwest),
blacks were not admitted to the law school until 1950.
That was the year in which the Texas law denying admission of Negroes to the law school was held unconstitutional by the United States Supreme Court in
Sweatt v. Painter, 339 U.S. 636 (1950), a case that
presaged *Brown v. Board of Education*, 347 U.S. 483
(1954). The first black graduated from The University
of Texas School of Law in 1953.

In 1965, the Association of American Law Schools
established a special Minority Groups Project simply
to count the number of minority students, and to ex-
plore the reasons why minority representation in the
practicing bar was so small. The study found that 700
black students were enrolled in ABA-approved law
schools, representing 1.3 percent of total law school
enrollments. "But even that shockingly low figure
was inflated by including the 267 students in the
predominantly Black law schools (Howard, North
Carolina College, Southern University, Texas
Southern and, at that time, Florida A&M). The Black
enrollment in the predominantly White law
schools—the other 145 on the ABA list—was

somewhat below 1%, and showed no signs of rising."
(O'Neil, *Preferential Admissions: Equalizing Access
to the Legal Profession*, 2 U. Toledo L. Rev. 281,
300 [1970].)

In 1968, the Association of American Law Schools,
the Law School Admission Council, the American Bar
Association, and the National Bar Association joined
forces to found the Council on Legal Education Opportunity. The Council established the CLEO
summer program, in which disadvantaged students
(mostly minority students) with marginal admission
credentials were given special training designed to
test their aptitude for, and to prepare them for, law
studies. Individual law schools established programs
of their own. (See *Symposium: Disadvantaged
Students and Legal Education—Programs for
Affirmative Action*, 2 U. Toledo L. Rev. 277 [1970];
Ramsey, *Affirmative Action at American Bar Association Approved Law Schools*, 30 J. Legal Education
377 [1980].)

In 1969, the American Bar Association began, for
the first time, to compile statistics on minority enrollments. In that year, 2,900 minority students (4.4 percent of 68,000 law students overall) were enrolled in
the 145 ABA-approved law schools. Of these, 2,100
were black and 400 were Hispanics. However, only
500 of those 2,900 students were in the third year of
law studies; 1,550, or over 50 percent, were in the
first year of law studies, a clear indication that the law
schools had just begun recruiting and enrolling
greater numbers of minority applicants. By 1971, minority students had increased to approximately 6,500,
4,000 of whom were blacks. Significantly, the black

law-student population in 1971 equalled the then current black lawyer population in the United States.

However, the law schools' efforts at recruiting minority students coincided with the staggering increase in applications from highly qualified nonminority students. Many minority applicants presenting credentials that would have assured their admission five or ten years earlier—thus indicating that they were fully capable of doing law-school work—found themselves in the lower half of a burgeoning applicant pool. The law schools faced a dilemma. Many schools wanted to increase minority enrollments, but they also wanted to take advantage of the newfound opportunity "to create a more intellectually elite profession than ever before." (Raushenbush, *Law School Admissions, 1984-2001: Selecting Lawyers for the 21st Century,* 34 J. LEGAL EDUCATION 343 [1984].)

To assess the law schools' response to this situation, it is necessary to have an understanding of the admission procedures employed at most schools. While the procedures vary considerably in detail, in broad outline they are similar. (See Ramsey, *supra.*)

Let us consider a hypothetical school that has 3,000 applications but only 400 seats in the entering class. The first thing that must be understood is that the school will offer admission to more than 400 applicants. Just as airlines over-book their flights to take into account no-shows, so also must the law schools. Most candidates will have applied to several schools, and candidates with strong credentials are likely to be offered admission to most of the schools to which they have applied. Past experience may show that the "enrollment yield" (ratio of enrollees to admittees) is 50 percent for this particular school. If that is the case, the school must offer admission to 800 candidates in order to produce the desired 400 enrollees.

How are these 800 successful candidates selected from a 3,000-person applicant pool? An important tool in the process is the school's "Admission Index" or "Predicted First-Year Average" formula. Each year, the Law School Admission Council performs a validity study for every member school, producing a prediction formula that correlates undergraduate grade-point average and LSAT score with first-year grades. Thus the prediction formula gives appropriate weight to the grade-point average and LSAT components in accordance with the experience of successful applicants to that school in earlier years. Since the LSAT score is reported on a scale of 10 to 48, the school's Admission Index formula might be 10 × gpa + LSAT = Index. Thus a candidate with a 3.8 gpa and a 42 LSAT score would have an Admission Index of 80, whereas a candidate with a 3.0 gpa and a 32 LSAT score (the rough equivalent of a 560 score on the "old" LSAT) would have an Index of 62.

The prediction formulae, while useful, are not precise measuring tools. For example, the Admission Index produced for The University of Texas in 1985, which has a higher correlation coefficient (.59) than most schools' formulae, has a standard error of estimate of 4.4. What does this mean? Suppose that candidate C has a predicted first-year average of 75. Does this mean that C, if admitted to the law school, is likely to finish the first year of law studies with a grade average of 75? No. Picture a bell curve. Under the prediction formula and its 4.4 standard error of esti-

mate, two-thirds of the students with C's credentials
are likely to finish the first year with a grade average
between 79.4 and 70.6. One-sixth of such students
will have a first-year average above 79.4, and one-
sixth will have an average below 70.6. As is suggested
by the scattergrams from which the prediction formulae are derived, the Admission Index has the accuracy
of a 20-bore shotgun, not a squirrel rifle.

At most schools, the candidates in the applicant
pool are divided into three tiers. The first tier consists
of candidates with high Index numbers, which means
truly impressive credentials. Since academic prowess
is a major factor (actually, *the* major factor) in most admission   decisions,   these   candidates—perhaps   as
many as 400—are admitted after only a cursory examination of their files. Candidates in this tier are often
referred to as "automatic admits."

At the other end of the spectrum, the third tier of
candidates, are applicants who, relative to the competition, have no realistic opportunity of being admitted. Consider an applicant with a 2.4 grade-point average and a 26 (30th percentile) test score. The applicant's Admission Index is 50, and past experience will
have shown that candidates in this range cannot cope
with the rigors of a legal education and a highly competitive student body. If admitted, this applicant
would be, at best, a C student in an A or B+ student
world. (What constitutes a third tier candidate of
course varies from school to school. Candidates in the
bottom tier of applicants to a small and intensely selective school such as Yale or Stanford might find
themselves in the first tier at a school that is lower in
the pecking order.) Third tier candidates—perhaps

the bottom 800 to 1,000 candidates in the 3,000-applicant pool—are also handled summarily. To be sure, the applications are read by either an administrator or a member of the school's admissions committee. However, a cursory examination is likely to confirm that "this guy really is a C student," and that the file does not reveal any compensating factors which would justify selecting this applicant over 1,600 others with measurably stronger credentials.

It is the candidates in the second tier who present the school's admissions committee with a formidable workload. Of the 3,000 applicants to my hypothetical school, 400 have been admitted "automatically," and 1,000 third tier candidates have been culled from the process. This still leaves 1,600 applicants, all (or at least most) of whom present credentials which indicate that they would perform effectively in law school if given the opportunity. Which 400 of these 1,600 applicants should be offered admission?

At this step in the process, while candidates with higher Indices have a presumption in their favor, individual applications call for careful examination. Take two candidates, A and B. A has an undergraduate grade-point average of 3.5, while B's gpa is 3.3. Since A and B have the same LSAT score, A's Admission Index is two points higher than B's. But what does this really tell us? Actually, it tells us very little until we take a closer look at the applicants' files. Where did A and B go to college? Suppose that B was graduated from an Ivy League school or a major state university, whereas A ran on a slower track at a state teacher's college or a small Bible college. Doesn't that suggest that B may be the stronger candidate notwithstanding the lower grade-point average (and thus a lower predicted first-year average)? On the other hand, the LSDAS reports for the two candidates (summary transcript analyses provided by the Law School Data Assembly Service) may show that the mean gpa for all law-school applicants from A's college was 3.0, indicating that A ranked very high in his class, and also suggesting that A's college may not have succumbed to grade inflation. In contrast, the mean gpa figure for B's college was 3.4, indicating that B was in the bottom half of her graduating class. Doesn't this information operate in A's favor?

What do the candidates' transcripts tell us? The fact that B majored in Economics at a school renowned for its Economics department, while A graduated in Home Economics, may swing the pendulum back to B. On the other hand, perhaps the transcripts will show that, during the fall of her senior year, B took a course captioned Household Economics and a freshman English Composition course ("Marriage and the Family" is another favorite) in an effort to pad her gpa, while A took challenging courses outside his major and wrote his senior thesis on Microeconomic Theory.

Both A and B are eminently qualified to do law school work at a satisfactory level. If both of them could be offered admission (as would have been the case ten to fifteen years ago), there would be no problem. However, there are several hundred As and Bs in the applicant pool, all presenting nearly comparable credentials (but with considerable variations in detail), only a portion of whom can be admitted.

Now: Reread the last three paragraphs and note the

unstated premise of the discussion. In comparing A and B, the only factors mentioned were relative academic performance and LSAT scores. The discussion has been stacked. If this were the operating premise of the decision-makers, it would reflect a policy judgment that academic achievement and performance on the LSAT are the *only* criteria to be considered in allocating an important resource: the finite number of available seats in the law school. To be sure, for the 400-odd automatic admits to my hypothetical school, academic prowess *is* the sole factor in the decision. At least to this extent, the school's desire "to create a more intellectually elite profession than ever before" (Raushenbush, *supra*) is accommodated. But should this be the sole, or even the dominant, factor in *all* of the school's admission decisions?

At nearly all law schools, the answer is no. In part, this position is born of necessity. If there are only minor differences in the credentials of A, B, and many of their second-tier counterparts, unless the school opts to rely on statistically meaningless distinctions in Index numbers ("74s and above are in; 73s and below are out"), or resorts to flipping coins, other factors must be considered.

In greater part, the schools have seized upon the abundance of qualified applicants to promote other goals. Fifteen years ago, when the system was in transition from an open-admission procedure to a selective process, it became possible for schools to admit "the best and the brightest," and to deny admission to applicants who were academically weak when compared with the competition. But now, when so many applicants have the necessary smarts, and it is possible to choose among them, schools can select "the best *of* the brightest." The criteria by which "the best" are determined vary from school to school, and in many cases from admissions committee member to committee member within the school itself.

Let us return to the discussion of candidates A and B. An examination of their LSDAS reports, college transcripts, and LSAT scores reveals that both are qualified for law study, but says nothing about what kinds of persons they are, what activities they engaged in at college, and what life experiences they have had outside a campus setting. Personal essays (required by many schools) may reveal traits of creativity, insight, and character that work to the candidate's advantage. Letters of recommendation from teachers and employers may provide insight as to the applicant's ability, leadership potential, and motivation. When did A and B graduate from college; and if it was several years ago, what have they been doing in the meantime? Many schools give preference to candidates who have been out of school for several years, having found that maturity and perspectives gained in the work force make for a better, or at least more interesting, law student.

At another level, some schools give preferential treatment to children of alumni, and to faculty children or spouses. Others favor resident applicants over nonresidents (more often as the result of legislative mandate rather than by choice). Still others, seeing themselves as national schools whereas most of their applications come from candidates in their region, seek geographic diversity. An applicant from Alaska or Idaho has a better chance of being admitted to

Harvard or Columbia than an applicant from Massachusetts or New York with comparable credentials.

Diversity, whether it be geographic or ethnic, social or experiential, is a positive element in the educational process. Students learn from each other, and
students with diverse backgrounds and interests can
bring their different perspectives into discussions
both within and outside the classroom. Minority
students often contribute to that diversity, to the extent that they come from different backgrounds and
are sensitive to different social values or issues. As
noted by Mr. Justice Powell in *Regents of the University of California v. Bakke*, 438 U.S. 265, 317 (1978),
schools may seek "qualities more likely to promote
beneficial educational pluralism. Such qualities could
include exceptional personal talents, unique work or
service experience, leadership potential, maturity,
demonstrated compassion, a history of overcoming
disadvantage, [and] ability to communicate with the
poor."

Where do minority applications fit in the law school
admission picture? Aside from those who (along with
many nonminority applicants) fall into the third tier
and are culled from the process, nearly all of the
qualified minority candidates are in the middle tier of
the applicant pool—and in the bottom half of that tier.
In the late 1960s and early 1970s, when law schools
began reaching out to enroll minority students, this
was understandable. Many minority students were
the products of segregated and inferior educational
systems, and more than a few had attended predominantly black or Hispanic colleges. It was estimated at
the time that, if no special efforts were made to re-

cruit minority students, blacks and Hispanics would comprise less than 2 percent of the law school student population. (Brief for American Association of Law Schools, *Regents of the University of California v. Bakke*, 438 U.S. 265 [1978].)

There were expectations, or at least hopes, that this problem would work itself out in time, as more minority students attended, and were graduated from, stronger undergraduate institutions which were themselves engaged in affirmative-action efforts. Regrettably, this has not come to pass—at least not yet. The minority applicant pool has grown in size, as has the number of minority students whose credentials demonstrate that they can do law school work. However, the nonminority applicant pool has also grown in size and quality. A significant number of minority candidates who present credentials that would have resulted in automatic admission ten or fifteen years ago now find themselves in the bottom half of the applicant pool.

At many schools, only about 1 percent of the first tier of applicants (the automatic admits) are minority applicants. Current estimates are that, if all law schools made admission decisions strictly "by the numbers," without regard to the ethnic makeup of the resulting student body, the level of minority enrollment in the law schools, and ultimately the level of minority representation in the legal profession, would be around 2 percent. (See LSAC/LSAS National Admission Statistics 1981-1985.) Faced with this prospect, many law schools continue to apply admission policies and practices which result in minority applicants being offered admission even though non-

minority candidates with higher Admission Indices
are denied admission. Should that be the case? What
values are served, and what goals are fostered, by
such an admission policy?

One hundred and fifty years ago, Alexis de Tocqueville visited a very young United States. Upon return-
ing to France, he wrote his celebrated book, *Democracy in America* (1840, Vantage ed. 1945). Tocqueville
made several pertinent observations on the role of
lawyers in our society.

"In visiting the Americans and studying their
laws," he wrote, "we perceive that the authority
they have entrusted to members of the legal
profession, and the influence that these individuals exercise in the government, are the most
powerful existing security against the excesses of
democracy. . . . If I were asked where I place the
American aristocracy, I should reply without hesi-
tation that it is not among the rich, who are united
by no common tie, but that it occupies the judicial
bench and the bar. The more we reflect upon all
that occurs in the United States, the more we shall
be persuaded that the lawyers, as a body, form the
most powerful, if not the only, counterpoise to the
democratic element.

"Scarcely any political question arises in the
United States that is not resolved, sooner or later,
into a judicial question. . . . [T]he legal spirit is
not confined in the United States to the courts of
justice; it extends far beyond them. [Lawyers] are

naturally called upon to occupy most of the public stations. They fill the legislative assemblies and are at the head of the administration; they consequently exercise a powerful influence upon the formation of the law and upon its execution."

It is interesting that these distinguishing features of our society should have manifested themselves so early in our history. As in the 1830s, even more so today: Lawyers "are naturally called upon to occupy most of the public stations. They fill the legislative assemblies and are at the head of the administration; they consequently exercise a powerful influence upon the formation of the law and upon its execution." Lawyers intrude themselves at other levels as well. In the community through service on zoning boards, town councils, community action groups, bank boards of directors, and in lay leadership positions in churches and synagogues, lawyers are seen (and much more often heard) out of proportion to their numbers.

For better or for worse, lawyers exercise disproportionate power and influence at all levels of our society. Unless minority representation in the legal profession is increased beyond current levels, the result will be that white lawyers, and as a functional matter white lawyers only, will continue to occupy these positions of power and influence. Is this what society wants, or should have?

If the answer is No, what should be done about the situation? Who controls access to the legal profession, and thus determines the level of minority representation within the profession? At first blush, it would appear that this gatekeeping function is served by the

Boards of Bar Examiners in the various states. Aside
from a few jurisdictions that grant diploma privileges
to graduates of law schools within the state (where the
gatekeeping function of the law schools is apparent),
all states require that a person pass a bar examination
in order to be admitted to the practice.

However, I should hope that my paper has demonstrated that, in an era of selective admissions, access
to the legal profession is controlled, not by the Bar
Examiners, but by the nation's law schools. Yes, it is
necessary to pass the bar examination in order to become a lawyer. However, in order to be eligible to
take the bar examination, a person must have been
graduated from an accredited law school. And per-
force, in order to graduate from an accredited law
school, that person has to have been admitted to the
law school in the first place. The consequence is that
the law schools hold the key to the gate, just as the
medical schools serve the gatekeeping function with
respect to the medical profession. In the
end—although chronologically it is at the beginning—it is our nation's law schools that decide which
persons are going to be lawyers and, conversely,
which persons are not going to be given the opportunity.

But, the question might be posed, if minority representation is to be increased, doesn't this mean that
the law schools must grant admission to minority
applicants who are *less qualified* than white applicants
who are denied admission? If the question is posed in
that fashion (as it often is), the issue is skewed. The
response should be, "less qualified by what
standard?" It is true that such a policy will result in

(and has resulted in) law schools' granting admission to minority students with lower grade-point averages and lower LSAT scores than some of their white counterparts. But this is also true whenever the daughter of an alumnus, or a skilled debater, or a resident of Alaska, or a graduate of the Peace Corps, or a retired Army colonel, or a wheelchair-bound applicant is selected over another candidate with a higher Admission Index but with no distinguishing features. Interestingly, it is rarely suggested, in such cases, that the Admissions Committee has admitted a "less qualified" applicant.

The difficulty with the phrase "less qualified" is that it is only a short slide to "*un*qualified," an altogether different matter. Earlier, I made reference to a candidate with a 3.0 undergraduate gpa and a 505 test score on the LSAT. As I pointed out, that candidate would have been admitted to The University of Texas (and presumably to other strong law schools) had he applied in 1970. Since those credentials would have the candidate just below the median of his class, presumably he would have graduated and would now be practicing law, if not sitting as a judge.

But suppose that candidate applies to law school today, and he is black or Hispanic. Is he qualified for law study? We could hardly answer this question in the negative without casting aspersions on a significant portion of the practicing bar. But if the candidate is admitted to law school and his credentials place him in the bottom quartile of the entering class, isn't he likely to earn a lower first-year average than his classmates who have higher credentials? Yes, the probabilities are that this will be true. The Admission Index formula does have predictive value. The purpose of an admission policy that encourages minority applicants is to provide access to the legal profession. It does not, because it cannot, assure equality of performance while in law school. Once again, though, the candidate's Index score does reflect that he has the capacity to do law school work, to graduate, and to become a successful lawyer, however "success" might be defined.

Well, then; what proportion of our lawyers should be representatives of these minority groups? Since blacks and Hispanics represent 18 percent of our nation's population, should our law schools strive to ensure that 18 percent of our lawyers will be black or Hispanic? There may be some who advocate this position, but I assuredly do not.

How many, then? I don't think that question needs to be answered. The only issue that needs to be addressed is the undisputed fact that these minority groups are underrepresented in the legal profession today. As another commentator put it fifteen years ago, "There is no need here to define exactly what constitutes a 'shortage' or discuss the question whether the number of minority lawyers should be exactly proportionate to the minority population. The number of minority lawyers is now so small that there is a shortage by any definition, and we are obviously years from having to confront the question whether the shortage no longer exists." (Summers, *Preferential Admissions: An Unreal Solution to a Real Problem*, 2 U. Toledo L. Rev. 377, 381 [1970].)

Values and value decisions underlie any professional school's admission policies. To say that "we shall be neutral, and we shall consider nothing but grades and LSAT scores, combined in an arithmetic prediction formula"—and, happily, no law school that I know of is that mechanical in its admission procedures—itself reflects a value judgment that academic prowess (academic elitism, if you will) should be the *only* standard employed in controlling access to the profession.

I would hardly argue that the world, or even our small corner of it, is a better place because we have *more* lawyers. I do suggest, however, that the legal profession should not be a white man's preserve. Perhaps, at some future Law and Free Society symposium, it will be necessary to confront Professor Summers' question whether the shortage of minority lawyers no longer exists. I hope so. Until that day arrives, I would urge the law schools to continue to strive for pluralism in their student bodies, by continuing to admit qualified black and Hispanic law school aspirants along with their nonminority counterparts.

PATRIOTISM AS A UNIFYING FORCE

by

Andrew R. Cecil

Andrew R. Cecil

Andrew R. Cecil is Distinguished Scholar in Residence at The University of Texas at Dallas and Chancellor Emeritus and Trustee of The Southwestern Legal Foundation.

Associated with the Foundation since 1958, Dr. Cecil helped guide its development of five educational centers that offer nationally and internationally recognized programs in advanced continuing education.

In February 1979 the University established in his honor the Andrew R. Cecil Lectures on Moral Values in a Free Society, and invited Dr. Cecil to deliver the first series of lectures in November 1979. The first annual proceedings were published as Dr. Cecil's book The Third Way: Enlightened Capitalism and the Search for a New Social Order, *which received an enthusiastic response. He also lectured in each subsequent series. A new book,* The Foundations of a Free Society, *was published in 1983.*

Educated in Europe and well launched on a career as a professor and practitioner in the fields of law and economics, Dr. Cecil resumed his academic career after World War II in Lima, Peru, at the University of San Marcos. After 1949, he was associated with the Methodist church-affiliated colleges and universities in the United States until he joined the Foundation. He is author of twelve books on the subjects of law and economics and of more than seventy articles on these subjects and on the philosophy of religion published in periodicals and anthologies.

A member of the American Society of International Law, of the American Branch of the International Law Association, and the American Judicature Society, Dr. Cecil has served on numerous commissions for the Methodist Church, and is a member of the Board of Trustees of the National Methodist Foundation for Christian Higher Education. In 1981 he was named an Honorary Rotarian.

PATRIOTISM AS A UNIFYING FORCE

by

Andrew R. Cecil

"Cari sunt parentes, cari liberi, propinqui, famili-
ares; sed omnes omnium caritates patria una
complexa est; pro qua quis bonus dubitet mortem
oppetere, si ei sit profuturus?"

Cicero, *De officiis*

The Concept of One's Country

Patriotism is love and devotion to one's country.
Adam Mickiewicz (1798–1855), Poland's greatest
poet, when Lithuania (formerly a part of Poland) was
under Russian occupation and he was in exile, wrote:
"Lithuania, my native land, / You are like good
health. / A man learns to treasure you / Only when
he has lost you." Although the idea of one's country is
undoubtedly one of the most potent social ideas, it is
by no means a simple matter to define it. We cannot
be successful in the inquiry about what patriotism is
until we have achieved some notion of what we mean
by "one's country," and that has always proved a
difficult concept to define.

The memories of the place where one was born and
raised cast a halo of sanctity on it. A man has a pious
attachment to the familiar scenes of his countryside,
its landscape and its memorable spots and monu-

ments, as well as to the traditional events, habits, and institutions that formed the environment of his childhood. These affectionate ties and memories, which often cause a pang of nostalgia when they are recalled, flow into the sentiment of patriotism but do not give it its true meaning. The immediate dwelling place of an American is hardly his country, even if this dwelling place is a city glorified by such songs as "New York, New York," "Chicago," or "I Left My Heart in San Francisco." However happy a man may be to live in a glamorous city or a teeming commercial metropolis, we would belittle the term "patriotism" to identify it with such satisfaction.

Similarly, there can be an erroneous tendency to identify one's country with a region or even with certain geographical limits. For a Frenchman, is Paris the France he loves, or is it Normandy, where the landing of the Allied armies was the supreme event in the European campaign of 1944? Does a British subject feel his primary loyalty to his city, such as London or Manchester; to his region, such as Yorkshire or Suffolk; or to England or Wales? Is Switzerland the city of Geneva, where French is spoken on the shores of its beautiful lake, or the mountain valleys whose cultures are so diverse? However vivid the proverbial pride of a Texan in his regional heritage, temperament, dialect, and wealth, the sentiments that flow from his feelings about "his country, the United States," extend over a wider field, over a political and moral entity definable by its history, by its civilization to which he owes his economic and spiritual life, and by its accomplishments.

These feelings are stronger than ties of locality, language, or ethnic background. The love of one's birthplace and home is topographical, intertwined with personal affections and the comfort of living in a familiar world that provides safety and the other blessings which a friendly community bestows upon its members. These domestic attachments have only a small part in building the sentiment of patriotism, which is formed by historical, political, and cultural forces. Even religions which are supposed to be universal are captured by national sentiment and merge with patriotism by asserting harmony between their claims of universality and the objectives of the nation.

There is a tendency to direct the sentiments of patriotism into channels of admiration for a man who has become an idol. In tribal times the chief exercised paternal authority and his command was regarded as an expression of the common voice and interest of the tribe. When the tribe became a state, people rallied around a leader who enlisted the people's sentiments by identifying his ambitions with the fortunes of his followers. Patriotism became a passion of loyalty to a dominating figure.

Alexander the Great conceived of himself as a hero in the traditional Greek sense. He founded cities on Greek models wherever his army went. He believed that his mission was to make the world Greek, and Hellenism (devotion to the Greek way of life) was the product of his vision and enthusiasm. He affected the course of history and fired the imagination not only of his compatriots but of the world. Julius Caesar, also regarded as one of the great geniuses of history, by gaining the admiration of the army for his bravery in the battlefield and of the people for his civil reforms, established the Roman Empire by uniting the State and pacifying Italy and the provinces. Roman citizenship became such a source of pride and even immunity that the apostle Paul could claim that he was not subject to physical punishment because he was a Roman citizen by birth.

A highly prominent figure in the modern era, the emperor of France, Napoleon Bonaparte, was one of the most skillful of military leaders. He made France paramount in Europe, and this superiority bred in her a fierce patriotism. By military exploits France rearranged the map of Europe, and the Napoleonic legend of a liberal conqueror and a reformer at home was a potent factor in France's, if not Europe's, history. He consolidated the results of the French Revolution; altered the disruptive effects of the Revolution's principles, which were spreading abroad; and, wherever he conquered, profoundly influenced the condition of life of the people.

Patriotism should not be confused with the perverse, blind passion of violent self-assertion and ill will toward the world. The Nazi party "worshipped" the Fuehrer, who devastated the spirit of the country by arousing uncritical devotion toward himself, combined with hatred toward those who refused to surrender to his ideas of self-glorification and brutal aggression. In 1935 the German flag desecration statute was broadened to cover profanation of the swastika and other banners and symbols of the Nazi party. (The Allied Control Council for Germany, which assumed governmental power following the defeat of the Third Reich in World War II, repealed the section pertaining to the swastika and other Nazi symbols.)

The identification of country with government is misleading. Patriotism does not call for blind allegiance to a government that represents no public interest. George Santayana made the distinction between the country's actual condition and its inherent ideal when he wrote:

> "Where parties and governments are bad, as they are in most ages and countries—it makes practically no difference to a community, apart from local ravages, whether its own army or the enemy's is victorious in war." (*The Life of Reason*, Charles Scribner and Son, 1905-6, p. 171.)

When Hitler invaded Russia, Stalin, aware of the hostility of the oppressed citizens to him, the Communist party, and its secret police, embarked on an effort to inspire patriotic ardor by appealing to duty and honor in fighting for "Mother Russia" and fatherland. To enhance historical sentiments, high military decorations for courage were established and named for the famous Russian generals Suvorov and Kutuzov, who had faithfully served the tsar: one for Generalissimo Suvorov (1729–1800), who, never beaten, defeated the Poles and drove the French out of Italy; the other for General Kutuzov (1745–1813), who allowed Napoleon to enter Moscow and pursued him as the emperor made his disastrous retreat from Russia. Stalin launched the defense against the Nazis on a wave of patriotic sentimentality, the same sentimentality in which, before the war, he saw treason and dissidence, which he punished by mass murder.

Patriotism may also be driven from national courses by religious leaders who assert that their governmental policy fulfills the will of God. Khomeini and Qaddafi bring terror and fear to their lands and other countries—all in the name of Allah. As an act of patriotism they send children to the battlefield and terrorists throughout the world. They have eliminated their opponents and conducted jihad—holy war—against all who disagree with them. When a country is brutalized by a tyrant who demands patriotic ardor from his oppressed subjects, the sense of the boundary between good and evil disappears.

Patriotism is a natural, cultural force that channels our thoughts and sentiments back toward the fundamental point where our attachment to the religion, literature, manners, traditions, and other aspects of our native land originated. In its purest form, it by no means entails the negative aspects which we have discussed above. It would be a mistake, however, to consider patriotism as only a moral or sentimental attachment. Patriotism is a political passion, which may be a source of joy and also a source of anxiety—experienced, for instance, by those who are sent off to exile; a source of pride, but also a source of bitterness caused by acts of violence and oppression inflicted on an individual's native land.

There is no prescribed length of time for a passionate sense of patriotism to mature. Someone has said that only immigrants know the true meaning of patriotism. The Poles who came to this country to escape the Russian occupation and persecution, the Irish who escaped the horror and suffering caused by the potato famine, the Jews who escaped the organized pogroms in Russia, the millions of other immigrants who escaped the brutal contempt for human life that characterized the lands of their birth—all became patriots when they landed in the United States, the bastion of hope for those who sought freedom and the right to the opportunities that life could provide. Those who had been victims in their native countries, upon receiving the welcome, "Give me your tired, your poor, your huddled masses yearning to breathe free," renounced their allegiance to their native countries because there they had been victims of violence, terror, or economic hardship.

Patriotism should not be identified with the love of any given government. Since the birth of society, however, there has been a tendency for symbols to become the embodiment of nationhood, even to become revered idols. When a chief of a tribe, a lord in the feudal system, or a monarch was able to awaken or to cultivate sentiments of love, loyalty, pride, and belief in a country's intrinsic worth, he became a symbol of patriotism. Americans do not have a history stretching back to ancient times or the Middle Ages, nor kings or queens with whom to identify the essential components of their patriotism and their reverence for their country. In the search for symbols for our common life, we rally around the flag.

The Embodiment of Patriotism

Throughout the history of the human race, banners, standards, and ensigns have been adopted as symbols of power, prestige, and authority. Early in the history of this country, the American people, acting through the legislative branch of the government, prescribed a flag as symbolic of the existence and sovereignty of the nation. "The flag represents a living country and is itself considered a living thing." (36 USC §176 [j].)

The courts have described the flag as a symbol of national authority that serves as an emblem of all for which this country stands: liberty and justice for all; protection of the weak against the strong; security against the exercise of arbitrary power; and absolute safety against foreign aggression. As an emblem of freedom in its truest sense, the flag is a symbol of patriotism, of pride in the history of this country, and of the sacrifice of the millions who joined together to build a nation in which personal liberty endures. It stands for this country's long roster of heroic dead, for the story of the past, and for the promise of her future. As an object of patriotic adoration, the flag encourages love of the country among people.

The provisions of the flag code generally relating to the proper manner of displaying American flags are merely declaratory or advisory, with no penal purpose. They provide that during the rendition of the Pledge of Allegiance to the Flag, all persons should face the flag, and men with headdresses (except those in uniform) should remove them and hold them at their left shoulders, the hand being over the heart. Persons in uniform should face the flag, and render a military salute. (36 USC §172.)

The Uniform Flag Act and similar state statutes

make it an offense for any person knowingly to cast contempt upon any flag of the United States by publicly mutilating, defacing, defiling, burning, or trampling upon it. (18 USC §700.) The purpose of flag desecration statutes is to enforce respect for the flag as an emblem of national power and national honor. The act also prohibits the use of the American flag in connection with advertising or commercial purposes. (4 USC §3.)

In the early 1940s state statutes requiring teachers and pupils of schools to salute the flag as a part of daily exercises created a controversy over patriotism. A Pennsylvania statute entrusted school districts with the task of instructing the elementary public- and private-school children under their control in "civics, including loyalty to the State and National Government." (24 Purdon's Pa. Stat. Ann, §1511.) To fulfill this task of instructing public-school children, the school board of the Minersville public schools on November 6, 1935, promulgated the following regulation:

> "That the Superintendent of the Minersville Public Schools be required to demand that all teachers and pupils of said schools be required to salute the flag of our country as a part of daily exercises. That refusal to salute the flag shall be regarded as an act of insubordination and shall be dealt with accordingly."

Lilian Gobitis, aged twelve, and her brother William, aged ten, members of a group known as Jehovah's Witnesses, were expelled from the public

schools of Minersville for refusing to salute the national
flag on an appropriate occasion. They had been
brought up to believe that the salute to the flag was forbidden by the command of Scripture that forbids bow-
ing down to a graven image. (Exodus 20:4-5.) A federal
district court granted an injunction enjoining the
school district from prohibiting the attendance of the
two children at the Minersville public schools.

The United States Court of Appeals for the Third
Circuit affirmed the decree of the district court (108 F.
2d 638), noting that the beliefs of the Gobitis family
were remarkably similar to the position of Colonel
James Alfred Moss, who wrote extensively on the
American flag. In chapter 14, "Patriotism of the Flag,"
of his book *The Flag of the United States, Its History
and Symbolism,* Colonel Moss wrote:

> "Another form that false patriotism frequently
> takes is so-called 'Flag-worship'—blind and exces-
> sive adulation of the Flag as an emblem or
> image—superpunctiliousness and meticulosity in
> displaying and saluting the Flag—without
> intelligent and sincere understanding and appreci-
> ation of the ideals and institutions it symbolizes.
> This, of course, is but a form of idolatry—a sort of
> 'glorified idolatry', so to speak. When patriotism
> assumes this form it is nonsensical and makes
> the 'patriot' ridiculous." (Washington, D.C., 1941,
> pp. 85-86.)

The regulation promulgated by the school board, in
the opinion of the court of appeals, was an unconstitu-

tional infringement on the free exercise of religion as applied to pupils who conscientiously object to saluting the flag on religious grounds.

Upon appeal, the Supreme Court reversed the decision of the court of appeals. (*Minersville School District v. Gobitis*, 310 U.S. 586, 60 S.Ct. 609 [1940].) Justice Felix Frankfurter, speaking for the eight-man majority, stressed that the mere possession of religious convictions which contradict the relevant concerns of a political society does not relieve the citizen from the discharge of political responsibilities. National security, stated the Supreme Court, calls for national unity, and the flag is the symbol of national unity, "transcending all internal differences, however large, within the framework of the Constitution." The ultimate foundation of a free society is the binding tie of cohesive sentiment, and the flag salute is one of the means to evoke that unifying sentiment "without which there can ultimately be no liberties, civil or religious."

The flag salute, maintained Justice Frankfurter, is an allowable portion of a school program aimed at the utilization of an educational process for inculcating "those almost unconscious feelings which bind men together in a comprehensive loyalty." He rejected the idea that the Court should exercise censorship over the conviction of legislatures that a particular program or exercise will best promote in children's minds the loyalty and attachment to the institutions of their country summarized by the flag.

Since the guardianship of our liberties is committed to the legislature no less than to the courts, Justice

Frankfurter urged judicial restraint in matters of educational policy aimed at securing effective loyalty to the traditional ideals of democracy. The courtroom, he wrote, cannot become an arena for debating issues of such policy. To assume such authority would in effect make the Court the school board for the country. "That authority," concluded Justice Frankfurter, "has not been given to this Court, nor should we assume it."

Within a three-year period the Court did a complete about-face by changing its position on the constitutionality of state requirements of the flag salute. In the case of *West Virginia State Board of Education v. Barnette* (319 U.S. 624, 53 S.Ct. 1178 [1943]), Justice Jackson's majority opinion overruled the *Gobitis* decision, and two justices of the *Gobitis* majority made the unusual admission that the *Gobitis* case was wrongly decided.

On January 9, 1942, the West Virginia State Board of Education adopted a resolution containing recitals from the *Gobitis* case (". . . conscientious scruples have not in the course of the long struggle for religious toleration relieved the individual from obedience to the general law not aimed at the promotion or restriction of the religious beliefs") and ordering that the salute of the flag become "a regular part of the program of activities in the public schools." The refusal to salute the flag was regarded by the resolution as an act of insubordination that "shall be dealt with accordingly." A child expelled from the school was to be treated as unlawfully absent from the school and could be proceeded against as a delinquent. His parents or guardians were liable to prosecution.

(§1851 [1], 4904 [4], West Virginia Code, 1941 Supp.)

When children who were members of Jehovah's Witnesses were expelled from school for refusing to salute the flag, Walter Barnette and others brought a suit to the district court asking for an injunction to restrain enforcement of the regulation of the board of eduction. The district court restrained enforcement and the board of education brought the case to the Supreme Court. This case called upon the Supreme Court to reconsider the *Gobitis* case and to solve the conflict that arose between governmental authority and the rights claimed by the individual.

Mr. Justice Jackson delivered the opinion of the Court. At the very heart of the *Gobitis* decision, wrote Justice Jackson, was the Court's position that "national unity is the basis of national security" and that the power exists in the state to select appropriate means to attain such unity; consequently, such compulsory measures as the salute of the flag are constitutional. Justice Jackson rejected the proposition that national unity is the question in the flag-salute controversy. The problem is, he stated, whether under our Constitution compulsion as employed by the board of education is a permissible means for achieving such unity. Referring to efforts by totalitarian countries to compel coherence as a means to unity, Justice Jackson concluded: "Compulsory unification of opinion achieves only the unanimity of the graveyard."

The Bill of Rights, which guards the individual's right to speak his own mind, did not, according to Justice Jackson, allow authorities to "compel him to utter what is not in his mind." In defense of freedom of expression and of conscience, he made this often-quoted statement:

> "If there is any fixed star in our constitutional constellation, it is that no official, high or petty, can prescribe what shall be orthodox in politics, nationalism, religion, or other matters of opinion or force citizens to confess by word or act their faith therein." (319 U.S. 624, 612, 63 S.Ct. 1178, 1187 [1943].)

The regulation of the West Virginia State Board of Education as well as the *Gobitis* decision and the holdings of decisions which preceded and foreshadowed it were overruled; the judgment enjoining enforcement of the West Virginia regulation was affirmed.

It may be noted that before the *Barnette* decision five successive Courts and thirteen Justices left the question of flag salute within the permissible area of legislation and held that the requirement of such a school exercise was not beyond the powers of the states. The *Barnette* decision outlawed such legislation by a shift in the opinions of two Justices (Black and Douglas), who submitted a "statement of reasons for our change of view" since *Gobitis*. Whether future shifts will change the history of the flag controversy no one can predict. These conflicting decisions lead us to acknowledge the following principles:

1) We live by symbols, since they are an effective way of communicating ideas. The State speaks

through crowns, emblems, uniforms, robes, and flags; the Church speaks through the crucifix, altar, shrine, bended knee, bowed head, and clerical raiment. Loyalty to schools, universities, and political organizations is expressed through banners, colors, or designs. In Poland, the crucifix is an active symbol of opposition to the communist regime. When in March 1984 the prinicpal of an agricultural school in Mietno ordered crucifixes removed from lecture halls, a battle over the crucifixes sparked one of the most spontaneous demonstrations since martial law was lifted in July 1983. The students showed up in class with crucifixes hanging from their necks. Poland's bishops defended the crucifix as a symbol of patriotism and Christian culture. Symbols transmit traditions from generation to generation and call for respect, and therefore no one is allowed to show disrespect for a symbol, such as the flag, that may result in a breach of the peace.

2) Patriotism should spring from free minds and inspired hearts. We cannot legislate patriotism, but we should strive to make people want to salute the flag. Justice Jackson's position—that to believe patriotism will not flourish if patriotic ceremonies "are voluntary and spontaneous instead of a compulsory routine is to make an unflattering estimate of the appeal of our institutions to free minds"—may, however, be challenged. In *Hamilton v. Regents* (293 U.S. 245, 268, 55 S.Ct. 197, 206 [1934]), the Court unanimously held that since attendance at a state-maintained institution of higher education was voluntary, a student cannot refuse to attend courses that offend his religious

scruples. The religious worshiper, wrote Justice
Cardozo, "if his liberties were to be thus extended
might refuse to contribute taxes . . . in furtherance of
any other end condemned by his conscience as irreli-
gious or immoral. The right of private judgement has
never yet been so exalted above the powers and the
compulsion of the agencies of government."

3) The flag-salute problem confronts us with the
problem which Lincoln cast in a memorable paradox:
"Must a government of necessity be too strong for the
liberties of its people, or too weak to maintain its own
existence?" We can make no absolute choice of an answer in favor of government's strength or in favor of
the strength of individual freedom of thought. But it
can be justly stated that, although in a free democracy
the individual is the center of society, the subordina-
tion of the general civil authority of the State to religious scruples should not always take place.

4) There exist numerous general laws that offend
sectarian scruples and—though they exact obedience—have never been declared as unconstitutional
(compulsory vaccination, compulsory medical treatment, food-inspection regulations, and the obligation
to bear arms, to mention a few).

5) The flag as a symbol will continue to arouse
mixed emotions. To some it will continue to represent
our heritage and our hopes. To others the flag will be
only a doubtful substitute for adequate understanding
of our institutions. The controversy over the constitutional power of the State to make reasonable provi-

sions concerning the flag-salute requirement parallels
the controversy concerning judicial and legislative
actions and the importance of judicial restraint.

Chief Justice Marshall made the following analysis
of judicial power and its relation to our scheme of government:

> "No question can be brought before a judicial
> tribunal of greater delicacy than those which in-
> volve the constitutionality of legislative acts. If
> they become indispensably necessary to the case,
> the court must meet and decide them; but if the
> case may be determined on other grounds, a just
> respect for the legislature requires that the obliga-
> tion of its laws should not be unnecessarily and
> wantonly assailed."

In my book *The Foundations of a Free Society,* I
pointed out the change of attitude of the Supreme
Court toward a greater deference to legislatures as the
originators of a State policy and the guardians of the
general welfare. (The University of Texas at Dallas,
1983, pp. 136-137.) The Court has edged closer and
closer to the position that gives more latitude to the
State's police power and that exercises greater caution
in labeling regulatory statutes as unreasonable, arbitrary, or capricious. The doctrine of judicial restraint
stresses the duty to avoid unnecessary lawmaking,
and, as Judge Learned Hand expressed it, insists that
courts should not intervene "unless the action challenged infringes the Constitution beyond any fair dis-

pute." (*The Spirit of Liberty: Papers and Addresses of Learned Hand*, Alfred A. Knopf Inc., 1960, p. 278.)

Justices Holmes and Frankfurter were among the most illustrious and outspoken advocates of the judicial "most alert self-restraint." They steadily adhered to the principle which precludes a judicial tribunal from holding a legislative enactment (federal or state) unconstitutional and void, unless it be manifestly so. Under this principle, the flag-salute question remains within the social and political domains of government, outside the Court's legislative concern. Advocates of judicial restraint maintain that the legislatures are no less committed than the courts to guarding our liberties and that it is, as Justice Frankfurter expressed it, constitutionally appropriate to "fight out the wise use of legislative authority in the forum of public opinion and before legislative assemblies rather than to transfer such a contest to the judicial arena."

Justice John Marshall Harlan (1833-1911), appointed in October 1877 by President Hayes to the Supreme Court, on which he served for thirty-four years, wrote that each state possesses "all legislative power consistent with a republican form of government." Each state may by legislation provide "not only for the health, morals, and safety of its people, but for the common good, as involved in the well-being, peace, happiness, and prosperity of the people." Guided by these principles the state may in every legal way cultivate a feeling of patriotism toward the nation and encourage a like feeling toward the state. Love of the Union and of the state "will diminish in proportion as respect for the flag is weakened," Justice Harlan remarked in his opinion in the case of *Halter v. State of Nebraska.* (205 U.S. 34.) This decision, as we mentioned, was overruled by the *Barnette* decision.

In the *Barnette* decision the Court took the position that judicial action is always justified when liberty is infringed upon. Stated Justice Jackson: "One's right to life, liberty, and property, to free speech, a free press, freedom of worship and assembly, and other fundamental rights may not be submitted to vote; they depend on the outcome of no elections." Consequently the ceremony of saluting the flag, when enforced against conscientious objectors, is "a handy implement for disguised religious persecution," inconsistent with the First Amendment and "with our Constitution's plan and purpose."

In addition to the rule that no man can be punished for refusal to salute the flag or to demonstrate respect in any other form, the Supreme Court also established the rule that no one can be punished for speaking contemptuously of the flag by word or gesture. (Only contempt of the flag by public act or physical contact such as mutilation, defiling, defacing, or trampling is punishable.) In *Street v. New York*, Justice Harlan (1899-1971), the grandson of Justice John Marshall Harlan, quoted above, pointed out that the right to differ "as to things that touch the heart of existing order," encompasses the freedom to express publicly one's opinion about the flag, "including those opinions which are defiant or contemptuous." (394 U.S. 576, 583, 89 S.Ct. 1354, 1361 [1969].) This right to express derision and contempt includes the right to turn thumbs down at the flag, to stick out the tongue, and to salute the flag with a clenched fist. (*Parker v. Morgan*, 322 F. Supp. 585 [1971].)

The above decisions are based on the assumptions that the flag is a symbol of the government and that people are contemptuous of the flag in order to protest against the government. These assumptions are ill-founded. The display of a national flag may be a symbol not of adherence but of opposition to an existing government. When the freedom fighters of Hungary battled Soviet tanks, the national flags they carried were a source of encouragement and inspiration. In totalitarian countries patriotic demonstrators sing the national anthem and carry the flag of their country as an expression of their protest against oppression and loss of freedom (as currently evidenced by the protests of members of Solidarity in Poland, subdued under the ruthless yoke of the Russian-controlled government). The flag is national property. In the United States the flag represents its diversity in ethnic, economic, religious, and political groups. It represents not the government but our open and democratic society.

The flag in the United States, like the national anthem, represents the shared national heritage of the nation. It has never served as a symbol of government or as a trademark of Democratic or Republican administrations. Why, therefore, should the right to be contemptuous and even defiant of government be extended to permit individuals to be derisive and disdainful of the flag, when it represents our freedoms and the principles on which this nation was founded and has grown to greatness?

No rights of the individual are more important than those relating to the free expression of personality, and among them is the right of free speech. The right to share thoughts with others is essential to the dignity of man and to his intellectual growth. However, the right of free speech—as our courts on numerous occasions have stated—is not absolute at all times and under all circumstances. Freedom of speech is subject to limitations and to reasonable accommodation to other valued interests. There is a legitimate interest in applying these limitations to protect the integrity of the flag from disgrace in the public estimation and from being degraded and cheapened by defiant and disrespectful remarks and gestures.

The changes that constantly occur in our society have an impact on the courts' reasoning. Our society expects that the judicial process can be adapted to varying conditions without trespassing upon the responsibilities which our constitutional system entrusted to the legislative branch of government. Attorney General William French Smith has remarked that when "courts fail to exercise self-restraint and instead enter the political realms reserved to the elected branches, they subject themselves to political pressure endemic to the arena and invite popular attack." (*The Wall Street Journal*, April 17, 1984, p. 30.) Among the controversies that invite such a "popular attack" is the flag-salute debate.

Patriotism as a Virtue

The meaning of patriotism, a topic widely discussed, is also a subject of controversy. A hundred and

fifty years ago Alexis de Tocqueville wrote, "Nothing
is more embarrassing in the ordinary course of life
than this irritable patriotism of the Americans." They
believed, he noted, that the United States, as "God's
new Israel," was destined to serve as an example for
the corrupt regimes of the Old World. Criticism of the
new republic was limited to the quality of its climate
and soil, but "even then," observed Tocqueville,
"Americans will be found ready to defend both as if
they had cooperated in producing them."

In the history of our nation the passion of the patriot for his country has been presented in conflicting
ways. In 1846, John J. Crittenden (1787-1863), the
senator from Kentucky and one of the leading
opponents of the war with Mexico (who also opposed
the annexation of Texas), referring in his speech
before the Congress to President Polk's Mexican war
message, exclaimed, "I hope to find my country in the
right; however, I will stand by her, right or wrong."
President John Adams took quite an opposite position
in his speech on slavery and unjust war when he said,
"And say not thou my country right or wrong, nor
shed thy blood, for an unhallowed cause." G. K.
Chesterton, the English essayist and brilliantly versa-
tile man of letters, in his *Defendant* even compared
the principle "my country right or wrong" to saying,
"my mother drunk or sober."

Our schoolchildren also receive quite a confused
idea of patriotism when they compare Shakespeare's,
"Who is here so vile that he will not love his country?" with Bernard Shaw's "You'll never have a quiet
world till you knock patriotism out of the human
race"; and when they compare Charles Churchill's

statement, "Be England what she will, / With all her faults, she is my country still," with the statement which Boswell attributes to Dr. Johnson, "Patriotism is the last refuge of a scoundrel."

The apparent confusion is often caused by frenzied outbursts of emotion that cloud the real meaning of patriotism. It can be "the last refuge of a scoundrel" when for political reasons those who proclaim themselves patriots attack the patriotism of faithful public servants they try to destroy. They use patriotism as a tool, to use the words of Aldous Huxley, "that fulfills our worst wishes" then enables them to "bully and cheat, what's more, with a feeling that we are profoundly virtuous." On the other hand, it also can be the love that puts country ahead of self, as was described in ancient times by Homer, "A glorious death is his / Who for his country falls," and by Horace, "It is sweet and proper to die for the fatherland." In modern times this sentiment was expressed by the famous words of Captain Nathan Hale, "I only regret that I have but one life to lose for my country."

The anatomy of patriotism is complex, and we shall try to determine the principles we must live up to in order to deserve the name of patriot. What kind of virtue is patriotism? There have often been attempts to characterize and categorize the different types of virtues. In the New Testament, the Christian virtues are portrayed as a moral perfection that goes beyond the law. The Beatitudes array the moral qualities of humility, righteousness, mercy, purity, and faithfulness to duty even under persecution alongside the expectation of grace that may flow from these qualities. St. Paul's list of "the fruits of the Spirit" (Galatians

5:22) reads like a catalogue of the virtues: "love, joy, peace, patience, kindness, goodness, faithfulness, gentleness, and self-control."

According to Thomas Aquinas, virtue denotes some perfection of power and "the formal principle of virtue is rational good." The theological virtues of faith, hope, and charity are distinct from the moral and intellectual virtues. The values in the theological realm are ruled by God's truth and goodness and measured by the greatness of his omnipotence and loving kindness. This is a measure exceeding human ability, because the object of the theological virtues is God himself. The four cardinal intellectual and moral virtues, according to St. Thomas, are *prudence*, which "produces that goodness which lies in consideration of reason"; *justice*, which produces that goodness "which consists in what is due and right in action"; *temperance*, the virtue which "restrains and represses the passions"; and *fortitude*, the virtue "which produces a firmness of soul against all manner of sufferings."

All these virtues are important elements of good citizenship and patriotism. We shall limit our discussion, however, to three virtues which make patriotism distinct in the context of our times: loyalty, readiness to defend one's country and sacrifice oneself, and tolerance.

Loyalty

A. *Loyalty to the Nation*

Loyalty is taken here to mean a fidelity that emanates from love of and devotion to one's country.

There can be no double patriotic loyalty to two countries. The Declaration of Intention of aliens desiring to become citizens of the United States contains in part the following:

"I will, before being admitted to citizenship, renounce absolutely and forever all allegiance and fidelity to any foreign prince, potentate, state, or sovereignty, of whom or of which I may be at the time of admission a citizen or subject; . . . and it is my intention in good faith to become a citizen of the United States of America and to reside permanently therein. . . ."

The petition for citizenship contains similar provisions. A naturalized citizen renounces his loyalty to a foreign sovereign. While the loyalty of a naturalized citizen belongs solely to the United States, patriotism does not preclude legitimate interest in and sentiment for the culture of a country of origin. The culture, language, and history of many foreign countries are subjects taught and fostered in the educational institutions of the United States.

Loyalty is constructive and not egotistic. As the love of children for their parents has no hatred or bitterness toward others, so loyalty does not preclude the patriot's humanitarian interest in alleviating the suffering and poverty of other nations or in building a world of progress and stability. Loyalty does not preclude the patriot's interest in promoting adherence to the rule of law and human rights or in building democracy in developing countries. The unifying force of loyalty enhances the citizen's interest in the well-being of citizens in other parts of the world.

Many times American patriots have died for the freedom of others. The flow of clothing, money, and other commodities to the prisoners released from German and Russian concentration camps, and the help extended to Europe and Asia—including defeated enemies—to rebuild their economies and to provide a shelter behind which they could restore democracy and prosperity are the fruits of patriotic loyalty translated into powerful forces for good in the world. As Santayana pointed out: "A man's feet must be planted in his country, but his eyes should survey the world."

Violation by a citizen of his loyalty to his country, or treason, when directed against the United States, consists, according to the Constitution, "only in levying war against them, or in adhering to their enemies, giving them aid and comfort." (Art. 3 §3.) The breach of loyalty consists of two elements: adherence to the enemy, and rendering him aid and comfort. Chief Justice Marshall, in defining "treason" during the trial of Aaron Burr, stated:

"It is not enough to be leagued in the conspiracy and that war be levied, but it is also necessary to perform a part. That part is the act of levying war. That part, it is true, may be minute. It may not be the actual appearance in arms, and it may be remote from the scene of action; that is, from the place where the army is assembled. But it must be a part, and that part must be performed by a person who is leagued in the conspiracy. This part, however minute or remote, constitutes the overt act, of which alone the person who performs it can be convicted." (*U.S. v. Greathouse*, 26 Fed.Cas. 18, 21 [1807].)

Any American citizen who commits an act which weakens, or tends to weaken, the power of the United States to resist or attack its enemies is giving them the aid and comfort denounced by the Constitution as treason. Since the crime of treason, which is an aggravated felony, is defined by the Constitution itself, the Congress has no power to enlarge, restrain, construe, or define this criminal offense. In a nontechnical sense, however, loyalty is not achieved merely by not committing the acts declared by the Constitution to be treasonous. The common meaning of loyalty is allegiance to one's country; this allegiance is violated by the citizen's failure or neglect in regard to trusts, duties, and obligations that he, in his devotion to his country, is expected to discharge responsibly and to the best of his abilities.

The answer to the question of when the citizen's responsibilities are fulfilled depends upon accepted values in a given society. In Stalin's Soviet Russia children proved their patriotic loyalty by denouncing their parents to the secret police for "anti-communist sentiments"; in Hitler's Germany the citizen proved his loyalty by participating in an unparalleled destruction of human beings. In the United States we should prove our loyalty by preserving the rights and prerogatives of democracy and by adhering to the values instilled in our institutions and our traditions by our forefathers. In 1783, at Boston's first commemoration

of America's independence, patriot John Warren
warned that "every State must decline more or less
rapidly, in proportion as she recedes from the
principles on which she was founded." Since patriotism demands our loyalties, we would do well to heed
this warning.

B. Loyalty to the Government

The terms "country," "state," and "nation," although often used interchangeably, are not synony-
mous. The modern nation is a territorial society, the
cohesive power of which is provided by the sentiment
of nationality that derives from a common language,
tradition, culture, and customs, which change slowly
if at all. No nation can be a State unless it can exercise
an undisputed central authority over its own people.
The State can incorporate several nationalities, but
this incorporation does not always succeed in obtain-
ing a national unity. For instance, in 1917 the Serbs,
Croats, and Slovenes proclaimed to the world that
these three peoples constituted a single nation, and
that their future state would be called "The Kingdom
of the Serbs, Croats, and Slovenes." This kingdom after 1929 was officially called Yugoslavia. The spurt of
cooperation and conciliation failed, however, and the
kingdom experienced continuous political unrest and
repeated crises.

The State is a sovereign political unit which regards
its power and authority as supreme. The citizens give
allegiance to the State because its chief concern is
their welfare and the maintenance of stability and justice. Allegiance to a State does not always mean alle-

giance to any given government. Governments may use their coercive power to enforce their authority to oppress their own people.

The Hebrew prophets did not hesitate to rebuke kings for their avarice, for their exploitative use of power for personal gain, and for their disobedience of the commands of God. The early Christians proclaimed a conciliatory attitude toward the ruling power, but refused to let the State claim their total allegiance. On the strength of the Master's declaration, "Render to Caesar the things that are Caesar's and to God the things that are God's" (Mark 12:17), they acknowledged also God's claims upon the citizen, claims that cannot come under the State's authority.

Paul expressed a conciliatory attitude when he wrote: "There is no authority but by act of God, and the existing authorities are instituted by him; consequently anyone who rebels against authority is resisting a divine institution. . . ." (Romans 13:1.) We find similar advice in the letter of Peter: "Give due honor to everyone; love to brotherhood, reverence to God, honor to the sovereign." (I Peter 2:17.) In sharp contrast, the Book of Revelation, in response to the persecutions under the Roman emperor Domitian (81-96), voiced the anger of Christians in cryptic but rebuking terms by comparing Rome to "Babylon the great, the mother of whores and of every obscenity on earth . . . drunk with the blood of God's people and with the blood of those who had borne their testimony to Jesus." (Revelation 16:5-6.)

In our generation those who refused to surrender their conscience to the tyrants of Nazi Germany or Soviet Russia died in concentration camps and prisons rather than declare their allegiance to the rulers who defied God and demanded the "things that are God's."

The dramatic demand for unqualified loyalty imposed by the Soviet government on its citizens is described by David K. Shipler, the Moscow correspondent of *The New York Times*, in his 1984 book *Russia: Broken Idols, Solemn Dreams:*

> "I encountered the anguish of men and women fighting to carve out for themselves some small zones of intellectual freedom, and I watched a few of them slide into either compromise or bitterness, either succumbing to the system's stifling demand for complete loyalty or pulling back and finally breaking painfully with the country they loved." (Times Books, 1984, p. 4.)

C. Loyalty Oath

The Constitution prescribes an oath to be taken by the president (Article 2, §1) and provides that senators and representatives of the Congress, members of state legislatures, and all executive and judicial officers both federal and state shall be bound by oath or affirmation to support the Constitution (Article 6). Oaths of persons assuming public office to uphold federal and state constitutions and to discharge faithfully the duties of their office are traditional and seldom have been questioned. Following World War II, when federal, state, or local governments, in order to insure loyalty to the government, adopted programs that included a requirement of an oath of al-

legiance or loyalty as a condition to the holding of
public office, such oaths were challenged on a constitutional basis. The oath of loyalty and of nonsubversion was intended to guard the government against
the threat of communism and the dangers of subversion by Soviet Russia in its aggressive and imperialistic policies.

Since the concept of loyalty encompasses elements
of freedom of belief, expression, and association,
every challenge to a loyalty oath raised the issue of
undue infringement of freedoms guaranteed by the
First Amendment. The Constitution does not guarantee public employment, but it does not at all follow
that a city or a state may resort to any scheme for
keeping people out of such employment. The government has the right to seek means of insuring that only
loyal persons occupy positions of public trust and influence, and one of the means is the oath of
nonsubversion. On the other hand, the individual has
the right to be protected against encroachment upon
liberties which are preserved by the First Amendment. In loyalty-oath cases, the Supreme Court, ac-
knowledging the need and purpose of the government to protect itself against subversion, tried to find
a balance between governmental and individual
rights.

The Supreme Court has never ruled that
nonsubversion oaths are unconstitutional per se, but
in determining their validity the Court has applied
specific constitutional tests. While admitting that the
governmental interest justifies the mandate of an
oath, the Supreme Court adopted as criteria of the
constitutionality of a required oath of nonsubversion

the standard of clarity and precision, the knowing-conduct or *scienter* standard, and the factor of intent standard. Following these standards, the Supreme Court ruled that a Florida statute requiring each employee of the state or subdivision to execute an oath that he had not and would not support the Communist party was unconstitutional as a denial of due process of law. The statute was invalid for its unconstitutional vagueness since the oath said nothing of advocacy or of violent overthrow of state or federal government, and said nothing of membership or affiliation with the Communist party, past or present. (*Cramp v. Board of Public Institution*, 368 U.S. 278, 82 S.Ct. 275 [1961].)

Because of the certainty of its terms, an oath required of municipal employees as to membership in subversive groups within a specified period was held a valid regulation. Similarly, the Court stated that an ordinance requiring every municipal employee to take an oath that within a specified period of time he had not been a member of or affiliated with any group which advised, advocated, or taught the violent overthrow of the government of the United States or a state was a valid standard of qualification and eligibility for municipal employment.

Overly broad and sweeping oath requirements, concerned with too wide a range of conduct and association, may be too vague to satisfy the requirement for precision. The Supreme Court held that an Arkansas statute compelling every teacher, as a condition of employment in a state-supported school or college, to file annually an affidavit listing without limitation every organization to which he had belonged or regularly contributed within the preceding five years violated the due process clause of the Fourteenth Amendment. The interest of the government in the fitness and competence of those it hires to teach in its schools, stated the Court, cannot be pursued by means that stifle fundamental personal liberties. (*Shelton v. Tucker*, 364 U.S. 479, 81 S.Ct. 247 [1961].)

The knowing-conduct or *scienter* standard requires knowledge on the part of one from whom the oath is required, of the subversive nature of the organization to which he may belong. Deprivation of employment or other penalty for innocent association would be, therefore, a denial of due process. In the application of this criterion, the Supreme Court held that legislation which excluded persons solely on the basis of organizational membership, regardless of their knowledge concerning the organizational purpose, created a conclusive presumption of the disloyalty of one who had been a member of or affiliated with a proscribed organization and was, therefore, an assertion of arbitrary power. (*Wieman v. Updegraff*, 344 U.S. 183, 73 S.Ct. 215 [1952].)

Because of the certainty of its terms, the Supreme Court held that a state statute requiring that, as a prerequisite to having his name appear upon the ballot, every candidate for public office must file an affidavit to the effect that he was not a person who was engaged in one way or another in an attempt to overthrow the government by force and violence, and that he was not knowingly a member of an organization engaged in such an attempt, did not infringe the constitutional rights of a candidate for municipal office.

(*Gerende v. Board of Supervisors of Elections*, 341 U.S. 56, 71 S.Ct. 565 [1951].)

Another criterion of the constitutionality of a required oath of nonsubversion is the factor of intent. The Supreme Court has ruled invalid any oath requirement not taking the factor of intent into consideration. In an opinion of the Supreme Court it was held that an Arizona statute—which required state employees to take a loyalty oath but did not require a showing that a state employee was an active member, with the specific intent of assisting in achieving the unlawful ends, of an organization which had as one of its purposes the violent overthrow of the government—infringed on the freedom of association protected by the First Amendment of the Constitution, made applicable to states through the Fourteenth Amendment. Without specific intent to further illegal action, those who join an organization but do not share its unlawful purposes and do not participate in unlawful activities, states the Court, "surely pose no threat either as citizens or as public employees. . . ." (*Elfbrandt v. Russell*, 384 U.S. 11, 86 S.Ct. 1238 [1966].)

Consideration of intent to further unlawful aims was underscored in the suit brought by State University of New York faculty members challenging as unconstitutionally vague a state plan to prevent state employment of subversive persons. The Supreme Court stated that knowledge as to the subversive nature of an organization will not suffice to answer the requirement of due process without provision for a consideration of the employee's intent or lack of intent to further the unlawful aims. (*Keyishian v. Board of Regents*, 385 U.S. 589, 87 S.Ct. 675 [1967].)

The decisions underscoring the knowledge and intent factors seem to shift the balance the Supreme Court tried to obtain between governmental and individual rights in favor of the individual rights protected by the requirement of due process of law. The limitation of the oath to affiliations with subversive organizations *known* to the person seeking public office and the requirement for consideration of this person's *intent* to further the unlawful aims of the organization overlook the fact that the governmental right to protect itself against subversion must to some degree affect First Amendment freedom. Furthermore there is a reasonable assumption that the oath would not affect adversely those who renounced their allegiance and severed their relations with such organizations. Although the responsibility to resist every encroachment upon the individual's constitutional rights was vested in our independent courts, the very nature of national security negates any inflexible concept, since it varies with the necessities of the situation.

Readiness to Defend the Security of One's Nation

Ernest Hemingway, paraphrasing Horace's famous line in his *Esquire* article "Notes on the Next War" of September 1935, contended: "They wrote in the old days that it is sweet and fitting to die for one's country. But in modern war there is nothing sweet in your dying. You will die like a dog for no good reason." Is it true that those who lost their lives in the war with

Nazi Germany died for no good reason? Do the
fighters for freedom in Afghanistan, who are laying
down their lives in the war against the Soviet in-
vaders, die "like a dog for no good reason"? Does a
surrender to an enemy who exalts hate, tyranny, and
oppression and turns human beings into commodities
deprived of any dignity offer a better choice? Is the
life of a person living under constant terror of being
arrested and held incommunicado for months if not
years a better life than that of a homeless dog?

If by "pacifist" we mean one who seeks to abolish
war and to maintain peace, every man of sound mind
would be a pacifist. Each human life is sacred. Peace
is the common value and aspiration of the community
of free nations. Man's energies, talents, and intelligence are God-given gifts ordained for man's true
blessedness and not for his destruction. But when a
man's country is faced with an enemy that has a long-
range plan for world conquest and has a huge armed
force of highly trained men, is it not the duty of the
citizen to defend his country whenever such a necessity arises?

The State owes to its citizens the duty of protection. The citizens have a reciprocal obligation to render military service in case of need. The United States
offers protection to its people and in turn demands
from its citizens support and defense, by arms if need
be, of its Constitution and laws. The Supreme Court
has declared: "Whatever tends to lessen the willingness of citizens to discharge their duty to bear arms in
the country's defense detracts from the strength and
safety of the government . . . for if all or a large num-

ber of citizens oppose such defense the 'good order and happiness' of the United States cannot long endure." (*United States v. Schwimmer.* 279 U.S. 644, 650-651, 49 S.Ct. 448,450 [1929].)

No nation engaged in aggression has ever acknowledged its imperialistic motives. Instead it hypocritically claims that its military action is prompted by concern for the well-being, justice, peace, and prosperity of the people whom it subjugates. Does this mean that small and defenseless countries should be left as prey to aggressive powers or to violent minorities trained and armed by often remote dictators? The so-called Truman Doctrine—which called for resisting aggression however far from the United States—was a major change in the foreign policy of the United States. President Truman wrote in his memoirs: "This was, I believe, the turning point in America's foreign policy, which now declared that wherever aggression, direct or indirect, threatened the peace, the security of the United States was involved." The key words here are "direct or indirect" aggression and "wherever" security interests are threatened.

In 1961, President Kennedy described the defense of freedom in the world as "a long twilight struggle." In his concern over the threat of communist penetration into the Western Hemisphere, he stated: "I want it clearly understood that this Government will not hesitate in meeting its primary obligations, which are the security of our nation." In Great Falls, Montana, in 1963, two months before he was assassinated, President Kennedy again stressed our nation's international responsibility for peace in the world. This message seems to echo down the years. Referring to American soldiers stationed far away from our territory, he told the audience: "You must wonder when it is all going to end and when we can come back home. Well, it isn't going to end, and this generation of Americans has to make up its mind for our security and our peace, because what happens in Europe or Latin America or Africa or Asia directly affects the security of the people who live in this city, and particularly those who are coming after."

The Soviet military empire and its surrogates have since established control over Vietnam, Laos, Cambodia, Ethiopia, Angola, Afghanistan, South Yemen, and most recently Nicaragua. It continues to widen the path of the expansion of communist domination and revolutionary violence. By destiny rather than by choice, the United States has the role of the watchman on the walls of world freedom, freedom upon which our security and peace also depend. The old, extreme-right conservative version of isolationism called for a splendid isolation maintained by adequate military strength. The new liberal or left-wing isolationism calls for substituting diplomacy for military strength and is built on the illusion that totalitarian, imperialistic countries will respect the rights of the free world as well as those of developing and backward countries.

This kind of appeasement was rejected by the famous nineteenth-century liberal John Stuart Mill. The author of "On Liberty"—in which he apotheosized individual liberty—condemned slavery as a "crime and scandal to humanity" and strongly opposed isolationism and pacifism. In a letter to James Beal he wrote:

> "Every civilized country is entitled to settle its internal affairs in its own way, and no other country ought to interfere with its discretion, because one country, even with the best intentions, has no chance of properly understanding the internal affairs of another; but when this indefeasible liberty of an independent country has already been interfered with; when it is kept in subjection to foreign power, either directly, or by assistance given to its native tyrants, I hold that any nation whatever may rightfully interfere to protect the country against this wrongful interference." (John Stuart Mill, *Collected Works*, vol. 16, *The Later Letters of John Stuart Mill, 1849-1873*, ed. by Francis E. Mineka and Dwight N. Lindley. University of Toronto Press, 1972, p. 1033. Letter 799. To James Beal, from Avignon, April 17. 1865.)

Mill favored the interference of France in 1859 to free Italy from the "Austrian yoke," and the use of armed force in defense of the liberties of the peoples of the Continent who were struggling against tyranny. He deplored as a "national blunder" the renunciation in 1856 by England's liberal government of his nation's maritime right to seize all goods on merchant ships destined for the enemy, even aboard neutral vessels. When serving in Parliament in 1867, Mill called for the resumption of England's belligerent rights on the sea, not "on narrow grounds of merely British patriotism" but because "the safety and even the power of England are valuable to the freedom of the world, and, therefore, to the greatest and most permanent interests of every civilized people."

In 1983 the United States used its power to restore self-determination to the people of Grenada. Those who condemned this action and compared it to the Soviet invasion of Afghanistan ignore the fact that five months after the operation there were no American combat troops in Grenada, while almost six years after the invasion there are over 100,000 Soviet troops in Afghanistan. The Soviet empire cannot survive without aggression. Milovan Djilas, a close associate of the late Yugoslavian dictator Marshal Tito and a member of the Yugoslavian Politburo from 1935 to 1954, was vice president of Yugoslavia when in 1954 he suddenly left the Communist party. After long experience with communism in the Soviet Union and Yugoslavia, he wrote: "Soviet communism . . . is a military empire. It was transformed into a military empire in Stalin's time. Internally, such structures usually rot; . . . but to avoid internal problems, they may go for expansion . . . if it is stopped, the process of rotting will go faster."

Aggressive and subversive activities of an enemy must be stopped. Experience shows that the tide of communist subversion can be rolled back. One example is the success of the Truman Doctrine in Greece, where after World War II the Communists—supported by indirect Soviet aggression—were close to victory. With the aid extended by the United States, democratic forces in Greece succeeded in forming a parliamentary democracy. The Congress reacted favorably to President Truman's call when he warned: "The free people of the world look to us for support in maintaining their freedom. If we falter . . . we may endanger the peace of the world, and we shall surely endanger the welfare of this nation."

In the two world wars, millions of men sacrificed themselves in the great battles in the hope that our world would be rid of those who threatened others with the poison of hate and fear, but every war scatters seeds from which a new war may emerge. How can a third world war be avoided? Not by appeasement.

Winston Churchill spoke of World War II as an "unnecessary war." It could have been prevented. If all the nations that united to fight our common enemy in 1941 had been equally united when aggression was first started by Japan against Manchuria in 1931 and by Italy against Ethiopia in 1935, the subsequent German aggression would have been prevented and the war of 1939-1945 would not have taken place. Aggression is an act of infamy. Defense against aggression is an act of patriotism. There is a basic right to oppose both the use of military force by an aggressor and the use of subversion or surrogate forces (such as Cuban soldiers or guerrillas trained by the enemy) which seek to override a nation's right to self-preservation. Such self-preservation requires stengthening the democratic basis of a society, and not multiplying dictatorships, whether in this hemisphere or in other parts of the world. This can be accomplished by deterring aggressors who try to impose their will by force.

Patriotism versus Nationalism

Patriotism and a readiness to defend one's country should not be confused with nationalism as such. Partiotism is constructive. Nationalism as a unifying force can be constructive, but it can also be divisive and destructive. The history of nationalism offers convincing evidence that a distinction between patriotism and nationalism should be made.

The 1860s and 1870s represented the period of the fruition of the ideas of liberalism, which advocated economic liberty, individual initiative, private enterprise, free competition, freedom of trade, removal of tariff barriers, and hostility to governmental regulation of commerce and industry. The 1880s and 1890s featured a period of ascending nationalism that reversed the liberal policy of laissez-faire. The "national historical school" declared war on economic liberalism.

In Germany, the national state—the German Empire proclaimed by the Eisenach Manifesto of 1873 as "the great moral institution for the education of humanity"—accepted the responsibility for regulating and planning the whole national economy: industry, agriculture, and labor. In Britain, each of the members of the Primrose League (created in 1883 by a group of "young Tories") pledged on his honor and faith that he would devote his best ability "to the maintenance of religion, of the estates of the realm, and of the imperial ascendancy of the British Empire." The same nationalist reaction against liberalism was registered in Russia, France, Austria-Hungary, Belgium, Sweden, and the Netherlands.

What were the consequences of the development known as nationalism? It unified the citizens of one country with bonds of patriotic loyalty and devotion but also acted as a wedge splitting the nations of the world. Protective tariffs became the dominant rule on most of the Continent. Each nation tried to protect its industry and agriculture from foreign products, still expecting to have a free flow of its products to foreign markets. The reciprocity adopted by competing nations and frequent international tariff wars led to an outburst of national imperialism and its inevitable result, colonialism.

European nations, in their search for new markets, new sources of raw materials, and cheap labor, subjected the world to their domination. Imperialism and colonialism were nationalistic phenomena. The hypocritical argument that superior races had a mission to civilize inferior races did not obscure the real aim of colonialism—the enhancement of national prestige and the procurement of colonial markets. The German kaiser on one occasion stated, "God has created us to civilize the world." Lord Curzon wrote: ". . . the British Empire is, under Providence, the greatest instrument for good that the world has seen." (Kirby Page, *The National Defense: A Study of the Origin, Results, and Prevention of War*, Holt and Rinehart, 1931, p. 5.)

As a result of the resurgence of economic nationalism and national imperialism, by the end of the nineteenth century almost the entire world had been appropriated by European nations. Rudyard Kipling urged the Anglo-Saxons to take on the "White Man's Burden" even if their only reward proved to be the contempt of the "inferiors" they were trying "to serve":

> "Take up the White Man's Burden—
>   Send forth the best ye breed—
> Go bind your sons to exile
>   To serve your captives' need;
> To wait in heavy harness
>   On fluttered fold and wild—
> Your new-caught, sullen peoples,
>   Half-devil and half-child."

Nationalism became imperialistic not only in other parts of the world but also at home, within Europe. Agitation against minorities became fashionable in the last decades of the nineteenth century all over Europe. Germanization was instituted against Poles in Western Poland, Danes in Schleswig, and the French in Alsace-Lorraine. Russia crushed two Polish insurrections and oppressed Jews, Lithuanians, Ukrainians, Georgians, Armenians, and other minorities within the Russian Empire. In Spain the government was adamant against the autonomous movements of the Basques and Catalans. Britain denied "home rule" to the Irish because they represented the "inferior Celtic race." The superiority of the Aryan race (with which the Germans were predominantly identified) and the Teutonic race (to which the Anglo-Saxons belonged) was widely discussed. The white race was destined, it was often claimed, to conquer and rule the inferior blacks of Africa, the yellow peoples of the East, and the other "inferior" peoples of the world.

When we read now the exuberant expressions with which politicians, philosophers, anthropologists, and other social scientists tried to prove that their nations had a peculiar mission to civilize the world and that their nationalistic policies fulfilled the will of God, we should be reminded of the prophet Amos, who—disturbed by the voices of those who regarded Israel as a chosen nation and as a special servant of God among the nations—cried out in the name of the Lord: "Are you not as the children of the Ethiopians unto me, O children of Israel? saith the Lord." (Amos 9:7.) No nation or race has license—scientific or scriptural—to regard itself as rightfully superior to others.

Nationalism and its by-product, militarism, played a dominant role in inciting World War II. In Germany the generation of those who sang "Deutschland, Deutschland über Alles" elevated a new catchword, *Lebensraum*—a space in which to live. Hitler, the leader of the National-Socialist Party, in order to fulfill the dream of his compatriots for "more space" which would bring "a better life," annexed Austria, partitioned Czechoslovakia, and finally—by invading Poland—started the slaughter of World War II. Mussolini, craving prestige, invaded Ethiopia in the hope of restoring the "Roman Empire." Japan, searching for new economic resources, embarked on an aggressive policy of colonization in Southeast Asia.

Nationalism is complex and, because of its contradictions, difficult to define. It lies at the core of a citizen's zealous pride in his country, but it also lies at the core of the dictator's hideous dream of world conquest. It includes the yearning for a restoration of national freedom among the nations presently enslaved in Eastern Europe, but it also includes the vicious hatred of the Russian imperialists who oppress them—a hatred expressed in the merciless crushing of any upsurge of the spirit of freedom in the subjugated nations. Nationalism is the answer to the strivings of newly emerging peoples for their independence, but it also implants fear and suspicion, separating nations from one another and intensifying the menace of international conflicts.

The prominent American religious leader Harry Emerson Fosdick, portraying the dangers of nationalism, wrote:

> "The gist of the matter lies in the fact that the dogma of nationalism, as it has developed in the last two centuries, has become a competing religion. I think it the most dangerous rival of Christian principles on earth. The crucial conflict today is not primarily Christianity versus Buddhism or Christianity versus Mohammedanism, but Christianity versus nationalism, and until one has clearly envisaged that fact one does not understand the crux of our situation." (*The Christian Century*, January 19, 1928, p. 74.)

Arnold Toynbee, the great British historian, in a 1960 article "The Reluctant Death of Sovereignty," described the threat of narrow nationalism by identifying it with a cult which has become mankind's major religion. The god of this religion, he stated, is a Moloch to whom the worshippers will sacrifice themselves, their sons, and all of their fellowmen, if conventional war should escalate into a nuclear one.

Patriotism is unselfish, altruistic, putting country before self. Nationalism is self-interest. George Washington said that nations were not to be trusted beyond their own interest. What transmutes individual patriotic unselfishness into national egotism? Reinhold Niebuhr found the answer, paradoxically, in a loyalty to one's nation that is a high form of altruism. Loyalty "becomes the vehicle of all the altruistic impulses and expresses itself, on occasion, with such fervor that the critical attitude of the individual toward the nation and its enterprises is almost completely destroyed. The unqualified character of this devotion is the very basis of the nation's power and of the freedom to use the power without moral restraint. Thus the unselfishness of individuals makes for the selfishness of nations." (*Moral Man and Immoral Society,* Charles Scribner's Sons, 1932, p. 91.)

It is most encouraging that since World War II the world has changed and the conflict between universal values and the selfishness of nations has been, at least among free nations, considerably reduced. With a few exceptions, the "thrilling" adventure of colonialism has come to an end. The countries of the so-called Third World have undergone the process of decolonization and become independent and sovereign. Their problems are no longer problems of liberation from the yoke of colonizers but those arising from national responsibility and the urgent need of development.

In the realization of global interdependence, production around the world has been significantly internationalized, thereby increasing productivity and efficiency and making available the lower-cost and higher-quality goods that have improved the standards of living of peoples all over the world. The three decades that followed World War II marked a period of diminishing importance of boundaries between countries and of encouragement of trade, competition, and investment. Since this is not a perfect world, grave problems such as inflation, unemployment, poverty, hunger, and desperation still remain to be solved. There is, however, no reason why in seeking solutions to these problems the Free World—with its material resources, research capacity, technology, and management know-how—should revert to narrow nationalism and protectionism by raising walls of protective tariffs between nations to limit competition.

Faced with aggressive Russian imperialism, the nations of the Free World must base their policies on mutual respect and solidarity, realizing that their mutual interest demands unity. The regional systems of collective security represent the Free World's main barrier to Russia's imperialistic ambitions. The vital interests of countries desiring to live peacefully are common to all; solidarity, therefore, fulfills the indispensable condition of peace. Europe, economically restored after World War II, recognized this need by embarking on the path of unity. When the Common Market becomes a living fact by accomplishing its aim of creating a unified internal market similar to the one that exists in the United States, a united Europe will become not only an economic power but also a real political power. Europe may never dominate the world as it did in the colonial days, but because of the riches of its civilization it will continue to exercise a preeminent role in shaping the world's future.

The United States and Europe must concentrate their efforts on maintaining unity and on assisting other nations desiring to defend their independence and freedom. The unity of the world—faced with the threat of Russian imperialism—is a necessity and must remain a reality. Its purpose is to preserve the nations that participate in collective security, not to compromise or destroy them. The national security and welfare of a free and sovereign nation is closely linked with the strength and prosperity of other free nations in all parts of the world.

Pacifism

The responsibility for the preservation of national security raises the issue of pacifism. The word "pacifist" in its common use means one who refuses or is unwilling to bear arms for any purpose because of conscientious considerations, and who is disposed to encourage others in such a refusal. From the inception of the republic, religious objectors have been expressly or implicitly exempt from bearing arms. Claims based solely on disbelief in war as an instrument of human policy have been disallowed by our courts, and only those who have objected to service in war because of religious scruples have been exempted.

In the historic practice of excusing citizens from service in the armed forces, there has been a shift from a test based on membership in a denomination opposed to the bearing of arms to a test based on one's individual belief. The Draft Act of 1917 (§4,40 Stat. 78) extended relief only to those conscientious objectors affiliated with some "well-recognized religious sect or organization" whose existing creed or principles forbade members' participation in war in any form, but the attempt to focus on particular sects broke down in administrative practice. The 1940 Selective Training and Service Act (§5 (g), 54 Stat. 889) discarded all sectarian restriction. Under the 1940 act the exemption was afforded to those whose opposition to war was based on "religious training and belief," making it unnecessary to belong to a pacifist religious sect. In 1948, the Congress amended the language of the statute to declare that "religious training and belief" was to be defined as "an individual's belief in a relation to a Supreme Being involving duties superior to those arising from any human relations. . . ."

Interpreting the intent of Congress in removing the theistic requirement and in using the phrase "Supreme Being," the Supreme Court concluded that the Congress deliberately substituted the phrase "Supreme Being" for the appellation "God," which may have a myriad of meanings for men of faith. A sincere and meaningful religious belief occupies in the life of its possessor, according to the Court, "a place parallel to that filled by the God of those admittedly qualifying for the exemption within the statutory definitions."

Within the phrase "religious training and belief," therefore, would come "all sincere religious beliefs which are based upon a power or being, or upon a faith, to which all else is subordinate or upon which all else is ultimately dependent." (*United States v. Seeger*, 380 U.S. 163, 85 S.Ct. 850, 851-2[1965].) The

Court established one objective test, "namely, does the claimer belief occupy the same place in the life of the objector as an orthodox belief in God holds in the life of one clearly qualified for the exemption." (380 U.S. 163, 184, 85 S.Ct. 850, 863[1965].)

In 1967 Congress amended the definition of "religious training and belief" by deleting the reference to a Supreme Being and by providing that "the term 're-ligious training and belief' does not include essential-ly political, sociological, or philosophical views, or a merely personal moral code." (Section 6 (j) of the Mil-itary Selective Service Act of 1967.) The valid consci-entious claim to exemption had, therefore, to be based solely on "religious training and belief" and the word "religion" was not intended to be inclusive of moral or ethical beliefs.

The 1970 Supreme Court's interpretation of section 6 (j) in *Welsh v. United States* marked a dramatic change. The Court restated the requirement for con-scientious objection as follows:

"If an individual deeply and sincerely holds beliefs that are purely ethical or moral in source and con-tent but that nevertheless impose upon him a duty of conscience to refrain from participating in any war at any time, those beliefs certainly occupy in the life of that individual 'a place parallel to that filled by . . . God' in traditionally religious per-sons. Because his beliefs function as a religion in his life, such an individual is as much entitled to a 'religious' conscientious objector exemption under §6(j) as is someone who derives his consci-

entious opposition to war from traditional religious
convictions." (398 U.S. 333, 340, 90 S.Ct. 1792,
1796 [1970].)

After the *Welsh* decision the term "religious training and belief" may include solely moral or ethical
beliefs, even though the registrant himself may not
characterize these beliefs as "religious" in the traditional sense, or may expressly characterize them as
not "religious." Prior to the *Welsh* decision courts and
draft boards attempted to give special meaning to the
distinction drawn in the statute between "religious
training and belief" and essentially political, sociological, or philosophical views, or merely a personal
code. The plurality (four justices) opinion in *Welsh* removed the distinction that had been intended by
Congress.

The question arose, can a conscientious objector,
whether the objection be rooted in "religion" or in
moral values, seek exemption when he is opposed to a
particular war only and not against war as such? In the
case of *Gillette v. United States* (401 U.S. 437, 91
S.Ct. 828 [1971]), the Supreme Court dealt with
objectors who for a variety of reasons considered the
war in Vietnam to be unjust and therefore opposed
participation in that war. (Gillette sought exemption
from the draft; Negre, the other petitioner, sought
discharge from the army.) The Court found the claims
to relief from military service without merit since the
conscientious scruples relating to war and military
service must amount to conscientious opposition to
participating personally in *any war and all war*. Opposition to a particular war may more likely be politi-

cal than conscientious and may include an enormous number of matters relevant to such an objection, such as whether the war is defensive or otherwise, whether certain weapons are used, the place the war is fought, the cost of the conflict, and so on. Furthermore, the objection to a particular war is subject to nullification by changing events. For this reason a program of excusing objectors from a particular war may be impossible to administer fairly and uniformly. The Court ruled that there was basis in fact to support administrative denial of exemption (in Gillette's case) and to support the army's denial of discharge (in Negre's case).

The truth of belief in opposition to participation in any war at any time is not open to question; the question is whether the objector's beliefs are truly held. The sincerity of the objector is a subjective question, and objective facts are relevant only insofar as they help in determining the subjective question of sincerity. The best evidence of an objector's sincerity, the Supreme Court has held, is his credibility and demeanor in a personal appearance before the fact-finding agency—the local draft board. The members of such a board, coming from the registrant's community, are presumably better qualified than anyone else could possibly be to pass on the question of fact involved and to decide whether he is telling the truth about being a conscientious objector or whether this is a mere pretense put forward to escape military service.

The duty imposed on the draft board is to determine subjectively and objectively the sincerity of the individual's deeply held religious, moral, or ethical

beliefs. It is up to the courts to determine whether
the local board (and ultimately the appeal board) was
rational and sincere in disbelieving the sincerity of
the registrant's belief. The disbelief of the fact-finding
agency may be rational and honest even when the
facts, standing alone, are perhaps insignificant, but
when considered in context help support a finding of
insincerity.

A. *Modern Pacifism*

Traditional Christian teaching made a distinction
between public and private defense. St. Ambrose and
St. Augustine in the fourth century gave unqualified
approval to Christian participation in war and unqualified rejection of private self-defense. They also
argued that there is an obligation to defend others
when attacked, if such a defense is sanctioned by the
State. In deciding whether it is right to fight in a war,
they argued, it is necessary to determine that one's
country is acting justly, in reasonable self-defense—it
was thus that the doctrine of a "just war" arose. St.
Augustine commented in *De libero arbitrio* that "the
soldier in slaying the enemy is the agent of the law (in
war), wherefore he does his duty easily with no wrong
aim or purpose. . . . That law therefore, which for the
protection of citizens orders foreign force to be
repulsed by the same force, can be obeyed without a
wrong desire." Their position was that a Christian
should resist evil by the effective means which the
State makes available to him.

On the other hand, a Christian, according to the
tradition of St. Ambrose and St. Augustine, should

not save his life in self-defense at the expense of
another when attacked in a nonmilitary situation. St.
Augustine excluded a right to private self-defense by
agreeing with Ambrose's position that "I do not think
a Christian, a just and wise man, ought to save his
own life by the death of another; just as when he
meets with an armed robber he cannot return his
blows, lest in defending his life he should stain his
love toward his neighbor. . . . What robber is more
hateful than the persecutor who came to kill Christ?
But Christ would not be defended by the wounds of
the persecutor, for He willed to heal all by His
wounds." (*The Duties of the Clergy,* III, iv, 27.)

The acceptance in Christian ethics of military
service in defense of order was grounded in the ideas
of justice and of Christian love of neighbor. The same
idea of Christian love for one's fellowman prompted
the early Christian to deny the individual the right to
save his own life at the expense of another. In
diametric opposition to this traditional Christian view
is the position of modern pacifists who refuse to participate in war to protect their neighbors and country
but claim the right to self-defense for the protection of
their life and "coat." The weight of the noble tradition
of the great Christian writers who looked with
profound skepticism on any defense against violence
on grounds of self-defense stands in sharp distinction
to the position of modern pacifists.

The conclusion reached by these pacifists was strengthened by a number of court decisions that have verified
the right of individuals to be conscientious objectors
even when the individuals have admitted that they
would fight or kill in the interest of self-defense or to

save their families, homes, friends, or churches, or even in a war if they were convinced it was directly ordered by God (and thus "theocratic"). In *United States v. Lauing*, for instance, it was held that a draft board could not deny the status of conscientious objector to a man who admitted he would not fight "unless the lives of my family or members of my church, or my own life was threatened. In this case I would kill if necessary." (*U.S. v. Lauing*, 221 F.2d 425, 426 [1955].) In another case, "the appellant stated that he never claimed to be against war in any form, that he believed in theocratic warfare commanded by God, and unless God told him to fight there was no reason to fight." He was still granted the status of conscientious objector. (*Kretchet v. United States*, 284 F.2d 561, 564 [1960].)

A "conscientious objector" who admits that he will kill in self-defense or to save the lives of those dear to him but will not defend his country has no claim to noble conscience. When a person expects others to defend his life and material goods, he transmutes religious beliefs into selfishness—he puts his private well-being above the interests of his country and of his fellow citizens. Granting the promulgators of such selfishness the status of conscientious objectors exempted from military service is to rend the fabric of society and to deny the obligations that are entailed in the great ideals of citizenship.

B. "Excessive Pacifism"

In the current geopolitical situation the question confronting the free world is: Is a country that is threatened in its existence, its liberty, or its identity morally bound to repulse aggression by force even by using nuclear weapons? The Roman Catholic bishops of the United States tried to provide an answer to this question in their pastoral letter entitled "The Challenge of Peace." The Catholic bishops of France also gave an answer to this important question in their statement of the issue of nuclear arms and defense entitled "Win the Peace," which was approved by a nearly unanimous vote of 93 to 2 in support of the document.

The pastoral letter "The Challenge of Peace" acknowledges the rights of governments to defense once every means of peaceful settlement has been exhausted. Endorsing the theory of a "just war" or "limited war," the letter gives a strictly conditional acceptance of the doctrine of deterrence and the possibility of a "just war" waged with nuclear weapons. The conditions are: just cause, right intention, and last resort to preserve human existence and to secure basic human rights; competent authority with the responsibility for public order and power to declare war; comparative justice (that is, are the values at stake critical enough to override the presumption against war?); probability of success, to prevent an irrational resort to force or hopeless resistance when the outcome of either will clearly be disproportionate or futile; and proportionality—the damage to be inflicted and the costs incurred by war must be proportionate to the good expected by taking up arms.

The pastoral letter stressing the significance of the last two conditions comes perilously close to an endorsement of the concept "peace at any price." The widespread devastation—if not indeed the destruction of civilization—that would follow a nuclear exchange, states the letter, "would be monstrously disproportionate response to aggression on the part of any nation." Referring to the conditions of the "probability of success" in bringing about justice and peace, the letter questions whether "such a reasonable hope can exist once nuclear weapons have been exchanged." The condemnation by the letter of retaliatory action which would take the lives of people who are "in no way responsible for the reckless action of their government" brought the warning from European clergymen and statesmen that the political consequences of the pastoral letter would encourage "war and the subjugation of Europe," since it would make Europe helpless "against a potential aggressor or blackmail."

A diametrically contrasting position is expressed by the document "Win the Peace," adopted by the Catholic bishops of France. Admitting that the "West is also ailing," they stress that it would be "unjust to weigh the East and West on the same scale." The document recognizes the "domineering and aggressive character of Marxism-Leninism, which holds that everything, even a nation's hopes for peace, must be used as a tool for world conquest." Because of the intrinsic perversity of Soviet Russia, the French bishops issued a warning about the pressure exercised by Moscow on Western democracies "to enter the Marxist-Leninist sphere of influence" while Eastern Europe is kept in bondage.

The church has always recognized the right of

political powers to counter force by the use of force. Peace at any price, the French bishops conclude, "leads a nation to all sorts of capitulation. Unilateral disarmament could even encourage aggressive behavior on the part of neighbors by presenting them with the temptation of an easy prey." What the French bishops call "excessive pacifism" (*pacifisme à l'outrance*), in the effort to avoid war, can turn peaceful nations into the prey of other forms of violence not less terrifying than war—namely, colonization, oppression, and deprivation of freedom and identity. The French episcopal document concludes: "Beyond the means of life stands the question of the reason for living. For people and also for nations and for mankind itself that is a . . . matter of spirituality." It is a "matter of spirituality" whether to become an easy prey of an enemy seeking world domination and offering annihilation and slavery or to assume the risk inherent in nuclear deterrence. History teaches us that a constructive policy of legitimate defense serves the cause of peace and deters an enemy from initiating a war. The best way of preserving peace without sacrificing freedom is to have an effective retaliatory deterrent. The sage advice *Si vis pacem, para bellum* ("If you desire peace, be prepared for war") is not an idle refrain.

Tolerance

The third virtue that forms patriotism, as we mentioned earlier, is tolerance. In discussing this virtue, we are reminded of Mr. Justice Holmes, who first formulated the "clear and present danger" rule (in *Schenck v. United States*, 249 U.S. 47, 39 S.Ct. 247 [1919]). Under this rule the constitutional guarantee of freedom of speech and of the press does not prevail where the spoken or printed word creates a clear and present danger of bringing about a substantial evil which the government has the power to prevent. While patriotism is a quality of enormous importance to the well-being of a nation, its excesses or abuses may in a certain sense also represent a "clear and present danger" and bring about substantive evils as well. We have already discussed some of these abuses as they relate to narrow nationalism and imperialism. Another abuse of patriotism is its use as a club to attack fellow citizens whose opinions differ from our own. Such an abuse is tragic because it betrays the deepest sense of patriotism. As Governor Adlai Stevenson expressed it, "To strike freedom of the mind with the fist of patriotism is an old and ugly subtlety." (Walker Johnson et al., eds., *The Papers of Adlai E. Stevenson*, vol. 4, *Let's Talk Sense to the American People, 1952-1955*, Little, Brown, and Company, 1974, p. 52.)

When those who proclaim themselves patriots attack the patriotism of loyal Americans and faithful public servants, the result is substantive social evil. The welfare of our society is endangered when irresponsible attempts are made to destroy the harmony of society by seeing treason in all dissidence. The welfare of our society is endangered by those who by self-glorification, self-assertion, belligerence, and hatred impugn the motives of others and try to pressure others into surrendering to causes, however irrational.

Mr. Justice Jackson, concurring and dissenting, each in part, in the case of *American Communications Association v. Douds* wrote:

> "Communists are not the only faction which would put us all in mental straitjackets. Indeed all ideological struggles, religious or political, are primarily battles for dominance over the minds of people. It is not to be supposed that the age-old readiness to try to convert minds by pressure or suppression, instead of reason and persuasion, is extinct. Our protection against all kinds of fanatics and extremists, none of whom can be trusted with unlimited power over others, lies not in their forbearance but in the limitations of our Constitution." (339 U.S. 382, 438-439, 70 S.Ct. 674, 704 [1950].)

Nothing is more pernicious than the characterization by one's enemies of any suggestion of change or reform as "Communistic" or of the advocates of even moderate reforms as "Communists."

In a free society, no one can deny others the right to hold ideas that do not conform with their own. Our freedom will be lost if we are compelled to feel, think, and act in consonance with patterns dictated by those who by claiming a monopoly on rectitude and righteousness demand conformity, and castigate any deviation from canons which they have established. A nation grows in wisdom by constant scrutiny and reexamination of conclusions previously accepted.

Judge Learned Hand wrote: "Heretics have been ostracized, exiled, tortured, but it has generally proved impossible to smother them." ("Fanfare for Prometheus," *Vital Speeches*, 1955, p. 1073.)

Truth is discovered when all ideas have an open field for fair consideration. Truth is discovered not by resentment of all dissent but by trial and error. If one claims that his opinion is the voice of God and condemns all whose opinions differ from his own, then God has actually been left out of the picture. Mutual tolerance calls for holding to one's convictions but without absolutizing what is relative. Mutual tolerance is the inner light in which freedom lives and grows, it is the air from which man draws the breath of love for his country.

Pericles, in his speech of 431 B.C. commemorating the Athenian war dead, said: "The freedom that we enjoy in our government extends also to our ordinary life. There, far from exercising a jealous surveillance over each other, we do not feel called upon to be angry with our neighbor for doing what he likes or even indulge in all those injurious looks that cannot fail to be offensive, although they inflict no positive penalty."

Tolerance encourages us to think of America as an assemblage of free individuals with equal opportunities, equal under the law, rather than as an assemblage of interest groups—ethnic, sexual, and economic—having a special status, and "exercising a jealous surveillance over each other." There is no real freedom of thought if ideas are suppressed or monitored. Our Constitution gives freedom of thought the same security as freedom of conscience.

Loyalty, readiness to put country before self, and tolerance are the virtues embraced by people whose hearts are filled with love for their country. They are virtues reflected by courage, a sense of duty, and keen feelings of pride, honor, self-respect, respect for others, and the steady dedication of a lifetime. They are virtues that give a multiracial nation the sense of unity that is the basis of a free society.

WITHDRAWN